NEIGHBORHOOD KID

DON'T JUST MAKE IT OUT, MAKE IT BETTER

DAVID MCGILL-SORIANO

Copyright © 2025 David McGill-Soriano. All rights reserved.

No part of this book may be reproduced, stored in a retrieval system, or transmitted in any form or by any means—electronic, mechanical, photocopying, recording, or otherwise—without the prior written permission of the author, except in the case of quotations used in books, reviews, articles, essays, or scholarly analysis.

I am happy to send a free digital copy for public benefit purposes.

Independently published on Amazon KDP (officially an indie author)

Cover photo by Jerrios

DISCLAIMER

This is a memoir based on my recollection of events. While I have tried to be as accurate as possible, some names, locations, and identifying characteristics have been changed to protect privacy. Certain scenes may be dramatized or reconstructed based on my memory. This story is shared with the intent to honor the truth of my experiences in the neighborhood and the lessons they taught me.

CONTENT WARNING

This book discusses topics of violence such as homicides, suicides, assaults, collisions, terminal illness, and other related themes that may be activating for some readers.

CONTENTS

Foreword 5
Neighborhood Dedication 12
Common Language 13
Chapter 0 Introduction 16

PART I.
THE HISTORY OF THE NEIGHBORHOOD AND THE NEIGHBORHOOD KID

Chapter 1. Neighborhood Upbringing 22
Chapter 2. Neighborhood Gangs 32
Chapter 3. Neighborhood Hoops 50

PART II.
THE WORK OF THE NEIGHBORHOOD AND THE NEIGHBORHOOD KID

Chapter 4. Made It Out 72
Chapter 5. Made it Back 92
Chapter 6. Made it Better 114

PART III.
THE TRANSFORMATION OF YOUR NEIGHBORHOOD AND THE NEIGHBORHOOD KID

Chapter 7. Neighborhood Victim 144
Chapter 8. Neighborhood Bounceback 167
Chapter 9. What it Means to Make it Out 184
Chapter 10. How To Change the Neighborhood 194
Chapter ∞ Conclusion: Just a Neighborhood Kid 208

Acknowledgments	214
Afterword	218
Notes	221
Reading Guide - Neighborhood Kids	225
Writing Process (How I Wrote This Book)	228
Reviews	233

FOREWORD

By Teresa M. Gomez
Human Dignity Program Manager, City of Long Beach

I arrived in Long Beach, California, as a wide-eyed 4-year-old immigrant, holding tight to my parents' hands as they stepped onto unfamiliar soil with four young children and a single, unshakable belief: that the American Dream was real—and it was worth leaving everything behind.

My father's first job was washing cars at the Harbor Chevrolet dealership. It wasn't glamorous, but to him, it was everything. He showed up every day without fail, driven by a quiet determination not to give anyone a reason to doubt him. Eventually, his dedication earned him a promotion to auto mechanic. He was proud of that role, so proud that he'd take us there on Sundays after church. We'd meet the salesmen, visit his workstations, and then run through the lot pretending we were picking out our future new car. On lucky days, we were treated to free popcorn and hot dogs, simple moments that felt magical to us.

After years of trying, my father finally landed the opportunity he'd been working toward: a job with the Los Angeles County Department of Sanitation. When that letter arrived, it was like he'd won the lottery. At the time, I didn't fully understand why it meant so much, but later I realized it was a gateway. It meant stability, a chance to own a home, access to healthcare, and above all, a pension. To him, becoming a public servant wasn't just a job; it was a calling, a privilege, and a symbol of *making it*.

I share this because the day I became a public servant for the City of Long Beach was, without a doubt, one of the proudest days of my father's life, second only, perhaps, to the day we arrived in this country. His journey planted the seeds of service in me, and living out that legacy means everything. Like my father, being a public servant is an honor and a responsibility I never take for granted.

In my role as the Human Dignity Program Manager for the City of Long Beach for the past 28 years, I've had the privilege of working and walking alongside the families and young people as they navigate some of the most difficult challenges imaginable. Over the years, I've witnessed the weight of poverty, the trauma, and the heartbreak of violence. These realities are all too common in parts of our city, and they often dominate the narrative.

Too often, the strength of a community, the quiet victories, the growth, the moments of connection get drowned out by the noise of grief and violence. These stories, the ones that truly define a neighborhood, are left untold.

Early in my career, I worked as a Neighborhood Improvement Specialist. My job was about more than projects; it was about people. I helped plant trees, organized cultural celebrations, and supported residents in becoming leaders. It meant long nights at community meetings and early Saturday mornings spent picking up trash with volunteers. But it also meant building trust, forging relationships, and falling deeply in love with the community I served.

One evening in 2004, I was heading to a community meeting at the local Community Police Center. As I passed through the Washington Neighborhood, I noticed flashing lights near a middle school—police cars lined the street, and yellow tape blocked off a couple of blocks. Something in my gut sank. I kept driving, unsettled.

When I arrived at the meeting, I asked a police officer what had happened. He barely looked up and said, "Yeah...a kid got shot and killed. The good thing is that's one less gang member we need to worry about."

His words hit me like a punch to the chest.

To him, it was just another incident. To me, it was a child. A life. A story cut short. I thought of all the families I had met, their determination, their courage, their dreams. That boy was someone's son, someone's friend, someone who mattered.

Despite the challenges, the systemic barriers, and the moments like that one, where it felt like compassion had gone missing, I've witnessed something far greater: resilience. I've seen families, young people, and entire communities rise again and again, determined to build something better, to hold onto hope, even when everything seems stacked against them. That hope, that quiet strength, is what fuels me every single day.

I recall back to 2006, when I had the incredible honor of being part of something truly special, a project that didn't just build a playground, but helped bring a neighborhood together. It was the KABOOM! Project, and it left a lasting mark on the Washington Neighborhood and on me.

KABOOM! is a national nonprofit on a powerful mission: to ensure every child has a safe, fun, and inspiring place to play, no matter where they live. They partner with local communities to transform neglected spaces into vibrant playgrounds, driven by the belief that play is essential to childhood and to community.

This neighborhood project was at 14th Street Park, the heart of the Washington Neighborhood. The existing playground equipment had fallen into disrepair, was broken, unsafe, and unusable. But thanks to KABOOM!, that all changed. In one unforgettable day, over 200 volunteers, Frito-Lay employees, City workers, and passionate community members came together to build a brand-new playground from the ground up.

It was a long, sweaty, beautiful day. We drilled, painted, lifted, and laughed. We shared stories, snacks, and a common purpose. And by sunset, the park had been transformed, not just physically, but emotionally. When the first kids raced toward the new playground, their joy was infectious. Seeing their faces light up as they climbed, swung, and slid for the first time on safe new equipment, made every aching muscle and every drop of sweat worth it.

That day wasn't just about building a playground. It was about reclaiming a space for joy, connection, and community. It reminded me of the power we have when we come together with love and purpose. And I'll never forget it.

In 2007, I attended the grand opening of a new, path-breaking housing development in one of the most underserved and, at the time, most violent neighborhoods in Long Beach. It was a powerful moment, one I will never forget. The development itself was beautiful, offering a few families the chance to move into brand-new, affordable apartments. But what stood out to me was the new community youth center.

The center had computers, a clean space for kids to do homework, after-school programs, tutors for the kids, snacks, and, most importantly, it provided safety, a sanctuary in a dangerous neighborhood. I remember watching the kids' faces light up as they explored the center. For many of them, it was almost certainly the first time they had consistent access to computers or a space designed just for them. I will never forget the joy on their faces.

What I didn't know at the time was that one of those kids, one of those wide-eyed young people full of promise and hope, would grow up to become my colleague at the City of Long Beach and the leader of our city's Office of Youth Development.

I am awed by how life comes full circle. Seeing someone who grew up in that very vulnerable neighborhood now leading efforts to support and uplift young people across the City is more than inspiring, for it reminds us of what is possible when we invest in our communities and when we believe in positive futures for our kids. Everyone in every neighborhood has stories that deserve to be told, but sadly, these stories are not told. The book you are holding in your hands is more than a book. It represents a living, breathing, and hopeful testimony of what it means to grow up in an under-resourced neighborhood, where real challenges are faced daily, and yet, despite this, you continue to choose to fervently believe in the better, not just for yourself, but for all around you.

David's journey didn't occur overnight. It came with real sweat, sacrifice, and deep love for this place and the people who nurtured and loved him. I've witnessed David's growth over the years, from a thoughtful, determined young man full of questions into a leader with a clear mission, to a leader with answers and, of most importance, a leader who put his mission and answers into action. From our earliest conversations, it became clear to me that David wasn't trying to just "make it out," but was committed to *making it better* for those coming after him. To that point, he had a vision and idea that came to fruition...

David is the founder of a very successful nonprofit, Books & Buckets, a youth organization that focuses on academics, athletics, and advocacy, which serves and employs the youth of his community. The organization has helped advocate for thousands of dollars in local park improvements, secured funding for a community center, served hundreds of youth from Central and West Long Beach, and hired employees, in addition to developing bright young community leaders.

Although I am double David's age, he has taught me about consistency, commitment, and dedication to growth, growth in several critical areas, among them professional, intellectual, health, family, and the environment. These are but a few of the many areas in which he has enlightened me and many others. I have witnessed firsthand the sacrifices he has made, the long hours he has put in, and his unwavering love for and commitment to the community that raised him. I burst with pride as I recall his early mentoring, now seeing him as a City employee, David, the manager of Long Beach's Office of Youth Development.

Over the past year, David has taken a brave step, turning inward to reflect on his journey, thereby transforming his lived experience into a book. And yet his book, NEIGHBORHOOD KID: don't just make it out, make it better, is more than a book, for it's a blueprint. It's honest, raw, real, and a public call to action. It's a torch to be passed from one generation to the next.

David's book serves as a love letter, a challenge, and a promise all wrapped into one. For every young person who reads his book, may you see yourself in David's pages. May you also know that your story matters, that you matter, that your voice, courage, and commitment matter. That you, too, are a powerful neighborhood kid who can help shape what comes next.

David shows us that success isn't just about escaping difficult circumstances or leaving troubled neighborhoods behind. True success—the kind that creates lasting impact—is about reaching back, lifting others, and transforming the very places that shaped us. David didn't just rise above his challenges; he turned around, returned, and poured his heart into *rebuilding what others had written off*. He chose to invest in people, in community, and in possibility.

This is the legacy David has built, not just in brick and mortar, but in lives touched, futures changed, and hope restored. His journey is not just a story of personal triumph;

it's a call to action. A reminder that we all carry the power to heal, to uplift, and to create something better, right where we are.

When David asked me to write the foreword for his book, I was deeply honored. Because this isn't just a collection of memories—it's a playbook for transformation. It's a mirror for those who have struggled, and a light for those still searching. David's story will resonate deeply because it speaks to something we all long for: a sense of purpose, a path forward, and the enduring power of hope.

Read this book not just with your eyes, *but with your heart.*

Let it stir something in you. Because in David's journey, we don't just see where he came from—we see what's possible when love, grit, and vision come together.

And that, more than anything, is what the world needs now.

NEIGHBORHOOD DEDICATION

This book is dedicated to the Washington Neighborhood and all the neighborhood kids around the world who are trying to make their neighborhoods a little bit better.

COMMON LANGUAGE

Neighborhood kids will be reading this book. I wrestled with whether to simplify the language for them or challenge them to learn new words—ones to circle, look up, and pronounce. I am aware of the low literacy rates in our most impacted neighborhoods, so I decided it was best to challenge them.

Figuring out when to use neighborhood slang or proper grammar was a constant struggle. I struck a balance. You'll see a small portion of purposeful grammatical mistakes involving missing prepositions, articles, wrong verb tenses, or fragments. In those situations, I favored emphasis and authenticity to convey rhythm and style.

This glossary serves as a home base of common language for some of the neighborhood slang or big words thrown in there. Because to me, both are a form of slang.

Outta: Short for "out of." Gotta: Short for "got to" or "have to." Sum: A neighborhood way to say "something" or "someone." It's just faster and quicker off the tongue.

Bird: My neighborhood nickname. It was given to me by the big homie Vincent when we were playing basketball. I could always shoot the 3, and he said I looked like Larry Bird. So from then on out, I was Bird.

Neighborhood: When I say "neighborhood," I am talking about underserved areas disproportionately impacted by violence, poverty, and adverse health stressors. I try to limit the number of times I say "hood" because of its subjective, negative connotations. I recognize the realities of the neighborhood objectively, not as a permanent condition. I want people to put their arms around the neighborhood, not despise it or make fun of it.

Double negatives: In the neighborhood, people prefer double negatives even when the literal meaning is the opposite. If a teacher gets you in trouble for something you didn't do, you'd say, "I didn't do nothing." Technically, "didn't" and "nothing" cancel each other out, meaning you did do something. But what we really mean is, "I didn't do anything." The double negative just sounds better because it doubles down on the rejection of something. I include asterisks to acknowledge the grammatical mistakes while savoring the feeling.

Systems Change: shifting conditions holding problems in place. If you change a system, its components and parts are fundamentally different, ideally, for the better. Systems change should lead to dismantling long-standing societal issues.

Population-level Change: effects that occur across a large group of people. This can refer to everyone living in a neighborhood or city, focusing on broader outcomes for an entire population. A program may serve 30 youth, but what does that mean for the entire population of youth in the neighborhood? Those 30 youth could have been diverted away from violence. But how does that impact all the youth who live in your neighborhood? Population-level change focuses on the larger problem at hand.

Place-based: a focus on a specific geographical location. I use this term when referring to the focus on my neighborhood.

Revitalization: To revitalize something is to give it new life and health. Vitality represents peak health, and "re" means to bring it back and do it again. We use revitalization to signify the transformation of places in the neighborhood.

Gangs: There is no consensus on what the word "gang" refers to. A gang can mean any group of people with a shared interest. Gangs are formed out of camaraderie, protection, and belonging. But the term "gang" is often used as a negative label associated with criminality and violence. In the context that I use the term, I am referring to criminal street gangs, in cases where that negative label is justified. Those that are tied to drug trafficking, gun trafficking, human trafficking, and/or violent territorial claims.

Medium: A means of transmission, serving as a bridge in between. A connector in the middle of two points. I use mediums to signify the bridges from violence to tranquility.

Barrio: A Chicano term meaning "neighborhood." The word is used as a form of endearment for the community I grew up in.

Vecindario: Spanish for "neighborhood." A term often considered more formal than "barrio."

La vida loca: 'the crazy life,' often used to describe gang life. I first learned the term from *Always Running* by Luis Rodriguez when he described gang days in LA.

Carnal: An alternative to "brother," "dude," "homie," or "bro." A popular Chicano term.

También: also; too; as well

En serio: seriously; for real; real talk

CHAPTER 0
INTRODUCTION

Picture a chaotic intersection—cars tearing through, *vroom vroom*, gusts kicking up debris from recent crashes, faded white and yellow yield lines, and scorching hot asphalt. It was a place of cherished childhood memories and life-altering moments. That was Pacific and 16th Street, a notorious crosswalk in front of my childhood home.

Looking back, I never thought crosswalks would shape the course of my life. I was just a neighborhood kid, barreling through to get to where I was going. I was headed anywhere but here.

Flashback to the Summer of 2009. My homie, Izzy, and I were crossing the street off Pacific and 16th in our infamous Washington Neighborhood of Long Beach, California. The day was hot, with the heat radiating off the pavement, and no trees or shade in sight. Izzy was a little taller and older than me—recognized for his braids, known for always lying (even when he knew that you knew he was lying), and loved by me for his reckless spirit when it came to neighborhood adventures.

As we walked across, Izzy told me, "I can't wait to make it out, bro. I gotta get the hell up outta here. Get me a house in Lakewood or sum."

Lakewood was the local suburban town seven miles away, with nice houses, yards, and white picket fences. All my friends saw Lakewood as the place to be. The quiet streets and suburban utopia filled with cookie-cutter homes signaled an aura of safety and security, something we dreamed of.

I nodded in agreement, replying: "Who you tellin', man? We gotta make it out the hood, no option. Gotta get a full ride to dip out this dusty place."

Izzy topped it off: "Man, once I'm out, I ain't talkin' to nobody from here. Gonna be livin' somewhere clean as hell," as he tosses the empty Hot Fries bag over his shoulder. It landed on the cracked pavement, where faded grass struggled to grow.

You see, Izzy and I were 11 years old at the time. Just neighborhood kids with big dreams and red Hot Cheeto fingers. All we cared about were Shasta sodas, "hood" Chinese food, Hot Fries, and leaving the neighborhood that made us. Leaving the neighborhood that brought us together. Leaving the neighborhood where we shared so many funny memories.

We wanted to leave because it was dirty, dangerous, and destructive. A place where violence was second nature.

Former Long Beach Police Chief Robert Luna, later Los Angeles County Sheriff, called the neighborhood the most violent police beat in his 35 years on the force.[1]

He saw it everywhere: on the ground, in calls for service, and in crime data on shootings, homicides, and assaults. The numbers were clear: this neighborhood needed help. That's why it was the first neighborhood in Long Beach to get a gun violence response protocol.[2] It needed it. And that's why when the police department launched a door-knocking campaign to check in on residents, these neighbors were at the top of the list.[3]

But we didn't need data or police reports to know how dangerous it was. We lived it. Every day, we felt the tension in the air, the struggle in the streets. That's why we fought so hard to "make it out." Out of the shadow of violence at our heels. Out of a place where even cops didn't feel safe.

We thought we were better than the neighborhood and that it didn't deserve us. That we deserved a safer, healthier place to live in. And you know what? We were right. Well, partially right.

We did deserve a safer neighborhood. One with a healthy environment to help us grow. A neighborhood that lifted us up instead of keeping us in a constant state of fight-or-flight. But what we couldn't see through the fog of disarray was that we didn't need an escape to Lakewood or some other more affluent enclave. We didn't need to *just* make it out of the neighborhood. There was a chance to make the neighborhood better, healthier, and safer too. A place we wanted to grow up in and raise a family.

That message of making it better is what this book is about. This isn't just another memoir, self-help book, or social impact read. It's a story on transcending an ideology that has long permeated our neighborhoods, with the hopes of sparking a domino effect of neighborhood change across the world. A playbook wrapped in storytelling. This isn't just another book for the shelf. It's a timeless message to turn the tide on the neighborhood's destiny.

The tale will follow the journey of a neighborhood kid, myself, from the Washington Neighborhood, who was once laser-focused on making it out, but later learned that his efforts should make the neighborhood into what it should be. Focused on making it better. *Focused on making it what it always should've been.*

Part I focuses on the history of the neighborhood and my upbringing as a neighborhood kid. Part II delves into the work we accomplished in the neighborhood to make it a place we were proud of. And Part III focuses on reshaping the idea of "making it out" with frameworks to transform yourself and your neighborhood.

To deliver this message, I tell the story of how I took a stand on violence, poverty, marginalization, and disinvestment—and decided that enough was enough. Through these pages, I share how a one-hour bus ride changed my life, how I was run over by a car in front of my childhood home, and how a local youth can change the world by changing their neighborhood. I want the reader to feel like we are taking a walk in the neighborhood. Passing by the blocks of storytelling and frameworks to end up at the home of a neighborhood kid...and his beautiful, resilient community.

Because this neighborhood kid right here will be one of many neighborhood kids to anchor the transformation of our neighborhoods and ourselves.

In the hopes that one day, local neighborhood kids don't feel like they gotta "make it out" of this neighborhood or any other neighborhood *enduring problems it didn't start*.

(Izzy and I at the 14th Street basketball courts in 2018)

PART 1

THE HISTORY OF THE NEIGHBORHOOD AND THE NEIGHBORHOOD KID

NEIGHBORHOOD UPBRINGING

I was born and raised in Long Beach, California. My first day in this world began at Saint Mary's Hospital off Long Beach Blvd, down the street from the neighborhood. It's a hospital with a lot of stories, a lot of gunshot victims, and a lot of people who call the streets home.

Tale of Two Worlds

My mom, *ma*, Celia Soriano, is from Jerez, Zacatecas, Mexico. She immigrated to the States in her late twenties. A brave and grounded woman, she always taught me how to light that fire inside and keep it burning, even when it rained. She began her career at the age of 15 as a rural federal teacher in Mexico, securing a prestigious placement. She was the sixth of eighteen babies my *abuela* had. They grew up on the *rancho* in Jerez, a beautiful pueblo where you could find people dancing banda in the streets. However, her hometown wasn't always filled with joy and celebration. Family turmoil and the weight of raising her younger siblings pushed my mom to leave Mexico and take a chance on the American Dream. She immigrated to the U.S. without papers in pursuit of a better life. The road was tough from the start: She worked in childcare, cleaned homes, cared for the sick, and even worked at Winchell's

Donut House, where gunpoint robberies were a common thing. It took time, but she earned her bachelor's degree at Long Beach State and became a paraeducator with the Long Beach Unified School District, a position she loyally held for 20 years. She did all this despite English being her second language. My mom is a proud parent, the kind who stands up for her kids when they are dealt the wrong deck of cards. She never hesitates to spark a revolution, speak for the silenced, and stick it to the man.

My dad, Edward McGill, grew up in Southern California. He was a tall, strong, blond-haired, green-eyed White dude who taught me to listen to the world around me and be kind. Dad was an LA County foster kid, adopted and saved by the McGill family when he was six. They gave him his first and last name. His biological family, the Robinsons, was torn apart. His biological mom and sister suffered from schizophrenia, and his dad battled alcoholism. All forms of abuse filled their home, eventually leading him and his sisters into foster care. Luckily, Judith McGill fell in love with my Dad and made him a part of her family. My grandma Judith, the matriarch of the McGills, was a foster parent who dedicated much of her life to supporting kids from broken homes. Despite the stability adoption brought, my dad still battled mental demons that led to suicide attempts and being institutionalized at one point. Eventually, in his forties, he began slowly turning things around. He already had a bachelor's degree from Long Beach State, but then earned his teaching credential from California State University, Dominguez Hills. That led to a nearly decade-long career as a health science teacher at Dominguez High School in the Compton Unified School District. My dad was a goofy parent who made sure I was always laughing and eating my vegetables.

My parents first met at a gas station in Long Beach. My mom spotted a handsome young man, initially thinking he was much younger. She knew she had the juice to game him up. His car had a 'For Sale' sign, so she walked over, pretending to be interested in buying it. They struck up a conversation, exchanged numbers, and went golfing on their first date. They hit it off, and a few months later, whimsically got married in Las Vegas. About a year after, I was born.

Family of Five

The first few years of my life were all over the place. I had two older sisters, Lisa and Denise, whose father was from Mexico but was usually not in the picture. The five of us were a team. A family. In photos, we almost looked perfect. But beneath the surface, we were stricken by poverty and a tumultuous home. Our home was an interesting mix—a mom who mostly spoke Spanish, two daughters from an estranged father, a father-turned-stepfather raised in a traditional Western household, and then a new baby boy who was a mix of it all.

We lived all the way in Northside Long Beach, at the notorious pink apartments off Paramount Blvd, then moved to the Westside, into a little apartment off Santa Fe Avenue across the street from the taco place. We got lucky a few years into my early childhood with a low-income Section 8 housing voucher that landed us a rental house with a backyard. We only lived there for a couple of years, but that house was one of the nicest places I ever called home.

Our family of five was broken up real quick. My mom and dad fought constantly. The fights were serious and got physical. The cops and social workers kept showing up, asking us questions about our home life. My mom loves telling the story of how a social worker interviewed us kids behind a closed door, asking, "What does your mom feed you?" I was only a toddler, but I quickly responded, "Gorditas." I loved my mom's gorditas and was proud of it. Even with my proud response, the constant 911 calls and social worker visits led them to threaten my mom: "If we get called out here again, we're taking your three babies." The only way my mom could guarantee they were never called out again was by hitting the road. She shuffled us up into her van, put an end to the relationship, and went on the search to find a new place to call home.

We were essentially homeless for months. Everything we owned was stuffed in my mom's van or a storage unit. We bounced between beat-down motels off Pacific Coast Highway in Long Beach near the Washington Neighborhood or "sleepovers" at my Madrina's house on the Westside near Stephens Middle School. Mom looked everywhere for a place to live. At one point, she was sent to the Long Beach Rescue Mission homeless shelter. She walked up to the building with us three kids, but saw only men inside. Worried for her daughters, she turned around and left, not knowing there was a women's and children's shelter right across the street. After weeks of motels and "sleepovers," we got lucky: Mom landed a back house garage from her friend on the edges of the Westside off Santa Fe and Arlington, resting near the concrete walls that hid the train tracks. That place went from being a storage unit to a home for a family, of now four, to rest their heads.

The Dales

A year after my mom split, she went into a custody battle with my dad at the Compton courthouse. Dad won 50% custody, so I was sent back to share my time with him when I was seven years old. Before that, I was a straight-up momma's boy, and I got used to living with just her and my sisters. Honestly, I almost forgot about my Dad around that time. I dreaded leaving my sisters and becoming a part-time only child.

On my last night with my mom before getting shipped off to Daddy Day Care, I was crying hysterically in the back of our 1994 Ford Aerostar van. I begged my mom to let me stay with her and my sisters. "Mijo, no puedo hacer nada. Es la orden del juez," she said ("Son, there's nothing I can do. It's the judge's order.").

25

Moving back in with my dad was torture for both of us during those first few months. I would repeatedly cry alone on the cold floors of the bathroom, using the towels on the rack to comfort my eyes and the flush to muffle my sobs. To this day, towels bring me comfort every time I smell the scruff bristles rubbed against my face. One evening, my Dad just watched me cry in the living room all night. He didn't know what to do. I feel bad he had to deal with me like that—to hear his son say he doesn't want to live with him.

Meanwhile, at my mom's, we got accepted into the Springdales public housing complex, known as *The Dales*, on the Westside. It was the projects, and it was rough. Behind those prison-like walls, anything could go down. That's where I first got robbed, beaten up, bullied, and saw racial tension. The street gang West Coast Rollin' 80s Crips, a Black gang, ran The Dales. They broke into homes, taking whatever they wanted. I noticed they only hit the Latino homes. That's when I first witnessed the racial divide.

A year in, our home was next. Mom and Lisa were out, Denise was upstairs showering, and I was outside playing kickball. Out of nowhere, my friend Beto shouted, "Check it out, they're breaking into your spot fu!" I was just a little kid, frozen, watching these tall dudes kick down our door and rush inside. I didn't know what to do. They snatched my PlayStation, CDs, movies—anything they could carry. Beto and I just stood there, helpless, as they stashed everything in the trunk of a car and casually went back to the playground like nothing happened. We ran to the security guard out front, but he was even more scared than we were. He called the police, who took about 30 minutes to show up. They made their rounds, reporting everything, and gave us a shrug, as if there was nothing they could do.

That was one of my first real epiphanies. I kept replaying the scene of men kicking down our door and wondered: Why? Why did they do that? Why do people ruin life for others? Why do we go at each other's throats when we're all in the same situation in the same damn neighborhood?" It lit a fire in me, *no doubt*, though I didn't realize it until much later.

Mom wasted no time getting us out of The Dales and into whatever one-bedroom, run-down spot she could find.

The Washington Neighborhood

Our first stop in the Washington Neighborhood was a small one-bedroom apartment off Cedar and 17th. We had some great neighbors, Botin and Antagracia, who always looked out for me. Botin, a construction worker from Nayarit, Mexico, gave me a dollar or two from his Friday paychecks. I used that money for my go-to Snow Storm ice cream or BB guns. He hardly had any money himself, but always found a way to spare me some on payday. I'd run up to him on Fridays, excitedly yelling, "Pay day, pay day."

The alley near those apartments was run by the local gang of the neighborhood. My sister was friends with some of the guys in the gang, and I idolized them. They gave me all the cheat codes for *Grand Theft Auto: San Andreas* on my PlayStation 2. I thought they were the coolest people around, something to look up to as a young boy hoping to be a real man himself. With all the problems my family faced just trying to make a living, it's no wonder why I saw a counterculture as something to aspire to.

Gangs were a symptom of the problems our neighborhood faced.

Neighborhood Snapshot:

The Washington Neighborhood spans 156 acres between Central and West Long Beach. On the streets, it is known as the *Eastside* because it is on the eastern half of the 710 freeway. Its boundaries are Pacific Coast Highway to the north, Long Beach Boulevard to the east, Magnolia Avenue to the west, and Anaheim Street to the south—a couple of miles from the Pacific Ocean. About 9,000 people live in the neighborhood, including a significant population of undocumented families.[4]

It has one of the highest proportions of children and youth under the age of 25 in the city. Around 30-41% of residents in the neighborhood are under 18 years old.[5] It's also home to the highest proportion of Latino residents in Long Beach, with Spanish often being the dominant language when speaking to your neighbor. Around 82.5% of households speak a language other than English at home.[6] The neighborhood is 72% Latino and 15% Black.[2] The remaining 13% is a diverse mix of ethnicities, including Cambodian, Vietnamese, Korean, Filipino, White, Pacific Islander, Native American, and others. People are constantly moving in and out, so these numbers are always shifting.

The Washington Neighborhood ranks among the poorest 20% of areas in Long Beach, with a median household income that is up to $50,000 *lower* than in other neighborhoods.[5] Around 94.4% of Washington Middle School students qualify for free or reduced lunch, the highest rate for middle schools in Long Beach.[7] Up to 80% of families live below twice the federal poverty level, meaning they aren't just poor by Long Beach standards but on a national level.[5]

Many of the families don't even own the roof over their heads. Landlords leech off the entire neighborhood, with around 86-96% of residents in the Washington Neighborhood living as renters, often in substandard conditions; a big difference from Long Beach's average renter rate of around 60%.[7] The Black and Brown families in the neighborhood don't have any generational housing wealth to pass down, living as renters *their entire lives*. This is why Habitat for Humanity wraps its arms around the neighborhood, bringing affordable homeownership opportunities to an area that otherwise wouldn't have it.

The neighborhood also has one of the highest rates of residents over 25 without a high school diploma, ranging from 36% to 57%.[5] That's nearly half the *barrio* and one of the worst rates in the city. The neighborhood is also a food desert, lacking access to fresh food from farmers' markets, community gardens, or supermarkets. The shadows of neglect in the Washington Neighborhood served as the perfect breeding ground for the largest criminal street gang in Long Beach, the Longos, which operates multiple factions out of the neighborhood.[2]

The neighborhood sits in the tough 90813 ZIP code, which falls at the bottom of every positive data set and jumps to the top of every negative data set. It leads Long Beach in emergency room visits for adults and ranks second-highest for visits among children. It also has the highest rate of adults reporting poor mental health and the highest number of uninsured residents.[8] And 90813 has the lowest life expectancy in the entire city.[9] People get short-changed in their go-around of life.

The Washington Neighborhood carries an ironic paradox. On one side, it's rough—like the dark, scary alley you see in the movies. On the other, it's warm and welcoming, like a neighborhood bakery that's owned by a local family. You can smell the fresh bread and hear the ring of the entry door as soon as you walk in. The baker's son with the busted haircut and silver teeth comes out to greet you with a cheeky smile, asking: "Which one you want?" The neighborhood has several of these mom-and-pop shops, intermixed alongside the sketchy alleys that you better not walk down.

The sketchy alley was where the local gang spent a lot of time hanging out. Nowadays, when I ask about what happened to those gang members in that alley, I am told they are all either locked up or dead. But back then, I looked up to them because that was all I knew. All I knew at the time was my block, my neighborhood, and my school. I didn't go on many adventures outside of it. I also thought it was cool to be part of a club that goes against the rules. Many young men find refuge, a sense of family, belonging, protection, and support within their local criminal street gang. The rite of passage of becoming a man is found in "putting on for the set" and proving your recklessness and aggression. When I was in 3rd grade, I wanted to join them. It was the peak of my desire to join a gang. I had a friend at school who was interested in the same path, and his big brother was in a gang. We even created our own wannabe gang at school. That friend of mine eventually joined a real criminal street gang.

But the avenues on my street led me on a whole different road.

(Mom and Dad at their marriage celebration in 1996)

(The family of five in 1998)

(The Washington Neighborhood in front of Washington Middle School—Books & Buckets Photo by Daniel Perez)

CHAPTER 2

My earliest memories of street gangs come from the alley behind our home off Cedar and 17th. I never really knew what they were doing over there. I just knew people called it "bad" and that I was supposed to stay away. But just like that time my dumbass almost burnt down the entire block after being told not to play with fire, there's something about wanting to do what you're told you shouldn't do.

Junior Gang

In third grade, I developed the aspiring identity of a future gang member. I was always scared of what it really entailed, more so the getting jumped in part, but I had a keen interest in the respect and power of it all. My homie and I started acting like we were a junior gang in training wheels. Every kid who wanted to hang out with us had to fight someone or do something bad; it was their initiation. We had little missions around campus that we'd do while skipping class. We even had our little kick-it spot behind the stairs where no one could find us. We were the toughest guys in the world.

My homie's brother was an actual gang member at the time, so he had the blueprint of how to act. And my older sister was hanging around with the gang who kicked it in our alley. She even started dressing like a chola—hair spray, McDonald's eyebrows, lip outlining, and puffed-up socks in her Converse. She was the coolest thing around. And she could beat me up, too.

But the street gang lifestyle couldn't keep its grip on me after my homie and I were split up. You could say I never had it in me or that the positive influences around me outweighed the pull. Some former gang members who do community work see that as a disadvantage for me in addressing gang violence. They have told me that I don't have the lived experience to prevent youth from joining gangs. Ironically, I do have the experience of what life looks like when you steer away from *la vida loca*. They drove over the trap. I was able to change lanes.

Unified Road

Several pieces of the puzzle shifted me away from fantasizing about gang life. First, I was put in a new class without the homie who shared my interest in gangs. Second, my dad became strict about any hint of gang culture—from who I hung out with to how I dressed, styled my hair, and even the hand signs I threw up. Third, I found a new identity as a basketball player. And fourth, I found new role models in NBA players like Kobe Bryant and Steve Nash.

1. **Social Circle**
2. **Parent Involvement**
3. **Identity**
4. **Mentors**

Social Circle

You mimic the behaviors of those around. Your social circle will influence your character. We are walking sponges. Our actions are intertwined with who we spend our time with.

After all the trouble my friend and I caused in the third grade, the school separated us the following year. He found a new group of friends, and I had to rebuild my social circle. Losing him felt like losing a brother, but I didn't realize it was a blessing in disguise. I started hanging out with kids who were actually good students; they were also kind to me. All of a sudden, I didn't feel the need to prove myself as a tough, aspiring gang member. I was chillin' with people who won Student of the Month and who raised their hands in class. I adopted a new culture of class homies.

That shift sent my identity on a whirlwind ride. I went from hating school, bullying kids, and telling people to "shut the fuck up" or "suck my dick" (inspired by WWE) all the way to paying attention, getting good grades, and trying to please people. I wanted to prove that I could be a great student just as I'd been a great troublemaker. The Student of the Month award became my new goal, a way to show what I could accomplish when I put my mind to it. I started talking less in class, writing more, answering more questions, and getting good test scores. I was determined to fulfill my new identity. Eventually, I scraped by and won the award. I was so proud to show my parents. My dad even stuck the Student of the Month sticker on the back window of his 2001 Nissan Xterra SUV.

Parent Involvement

A once-a-week program can never compare to the influence of our parents. We often emulate our moms and dads, even when we don't want to. During childhood, your life's structure is at the discretion of your parents.

Once my dad realized the negative influences around me, he put his foot down. *Zero tolerance type.* If I showed any hint of gang-related behavior, he'd shut that shit down immediately. One time, he took me to get a haircut at Supercuts. I don't know what the hell he was thinking taking me there instead of a neighborhood barber, but that's beside the point. They hooked me up and gave me the spiky hair look. Just how I liked it. That was the cool look among grade school kids in the 2000s. But my dad associated it with gangs, so he sternly told the barber while waving his finger side to side, "No, no, keep cutting down to a military buzz cut."

Dad even got involved with the Parent Teacher Association. He'd inform my mom about school problems and keep an eagle eye on me. He also made sure I played sports.

I was scared of my dad, so his pressure weighed heavy. One incident stands out: In my fourth-grade class photo, I threw up the Jeff Hardy hand sign from WWE with my ring finger down. And then during our open house, he saw it on the class billboard. Man, he blew up. It wasn't the immediate yelling and scolding kind of way. That wasn't him. He would hold this stoic, silent anger, where I had to wait until he was ready to say something. It was terrifying not knowing when it was coming. I would just want to get it over with instead of it hovering above me like a cloud of water waiting to release the rain. The talk, when he was ready, was always calm and stern. "I don't want to see my son throwing up any hand signs," he said.

"But Dad, it was the Spiderman sign, I..."

"I don't want to hear it, do you understand?" he interrupted.

I knew he didn't like me watching wrestling, so I lied and said it was a superhero. It wasn't a gang sign, but I got the message.

Identity

The self-fulfilling prophecy maintains that we will fulfill the prophecy we place on ourselves or the ones placed on us. We are constantly role-playing throughout our lives. We subconsciously step into our identities based on environment, experience, and external labels.

When the beautiful game of basketball entered my life, it was love at first sight. I was naturally good at it. I could shoot that ball better than anyone on the court. For some reason, when I threw that thing in the air, it was straight money. One of my dad's favorite memories was me yelling, "Dad look, Kobe!" while dribbling it between my legs and throwing it over my shoulder for nothing but net, followed by a well-earned high-five. Basketball became my sole focus when my dad put me in a Parks & Rec league. At 9 years old, I hit a buzzer-beater to win a game with six seconds left. The crowd went crazy, shaking the walls and hardwood floors. I became obsessed after that. I loved the energy of the crowd and all the praise they gave. The juice of competition and success. I wanted to relive that. It was a drug. And I was hooked. I switched out my fascination with gangs for the game of basketball. Playing in the NBA was all I cared about. It was my new identity. I was a basketball player, determined to be the best.

Mentors

There are always giants who came before us. We look up to them. We use them as inspiration and direction for the life we want to live. Mentors serve as those giants.

My newfound love of basketball opened the door to positive mentors in my life. At the time, Kobe Bryant was the man. He had just won MVP, dominated the Olympics with a clutch Gold medal game, and then followed up with an NBA championship without Shaq. Kobe was the best basketball player in the world. I loved watching how ice-cold he was in clutch moments; I was nervous just watching from our couch. I used to watch the Lakers on KCAL9 with a small box TV. Watching Kobe play became my study hall. I practiced all of his fadeaway shots, yelling out "Kooobbbeee!"

Steve Nash was another mentor for me. The Phoenix Suns, at one point, were the Lakers' kryptonite. No one set the tone of the game like Nash. He was smooth with the passes and dimes, and he hardly missed. Learning from the greats of Kobe Bryant and Steve Nash was my form of mentorship, even though I never met them. I looked up to them as adults I could turn to for advice.

All these factors—social circle, parent involvement, identity, and mentors—paved a unified road away from gang life. Although I never became a gang member, I was still fascinated by the culture. As I got older, I started studying why I didn't join a gang and why my community was set up to push young men to give up their lives for gangs.

Block Life

Many gang members die over the territory they claim. Joining a gang has even been compared to committing suicide. Throwing yourself in situations where you might get shot or stabbed isn't the same as jumping off a bridge or hanging yourself in a room, but it still puts your life at a high risk of death. Many gang members intentionally do this to "put on for the set." If you join a gang at 14 and don't expect to live past 21 because you are ready to put your life on the line, then that's similar to crafting your own funeral. It's a delayed suicide. You are sacrificing your youth for a social construct: a claimed territory that isn't even yours. You don't decide which buildings are built or which businesses open up. The territorial claim is a fantasy.

I remember speaking to a former Eastside Longo gang member who said his world didn't extend beyond his block. That was his universe. To him, the world began and ended on his busted-up block. He'd never traveled, camped, swum, or hiked. The block was all he knew, and that's why he was ready to die for it. Young men in gang-ridden neighborhoods need to be encouraged to explore the world beyond the confines of their blocks. They need to see how vast and beautiful this place is—to understand that dying for your block is dumb and that they can create their own destiny. This is why exposing gang-impacted youth to camping or traveling is crucial for deterring violence. As Eba Laye, founder of the youth-serving organization Whole Systems Learning, has reminded me, these experiences of exploration create new networks of thought and imagination for young, growing minds.[10] This expands their dreams and ideas about the possibilities in life. As my close friend Leonidas always says, "Exposure expands expectations." Organizations like Whole Systems Learning can change a neighborhood by uplifting expectations. But it starts with believing we can solve the problem in the first place.

I truly believe that gang violence can be solved, and when I was 24 in the summer of 2022, I was talking to a park supervisor at Seaside Park about it. They were setting up for a Movie in the Park night to activate the neighborhood. The employee had requested extra patrols due to the park's reputation for violence. I started talking about how we needed to solve the root of the problem so that one day, we wouldn't need the extra patrols. His response stunned me: He got defensive and told me in a manner like I didn't know shit, "Gangs have always been a part of this neighborhood, and they always will be. That's just the way it is around here."

He was asking me to normalize violence among children, families, and communities. He was insinuating that I should lose hope in the dream of a peaceful neighborhood. Easy to say when you don't have to live it. He got to drive away from the neighborhood after every shift, leaving the problems for another day. I didn't waste my time responding to him as I was lost in disbelief, and honestly, *it fired me up.* That night, there was a shooting in the neighborhood, which caused a helicopter to comb through the area with its blinding light flashing down on families watching the movie. It was a frustrating reminder of the violence, but I knew it wasn't always this way.

History of Gangs

Criminal street gangs haven't always existed in my neighborhood. The earliest history of gangs in the United States dates back to New York after the American Revolution, with gangs such as the Dead Rabbits. These early gangs, made up of European immigrants, were created after an influx of immigration and overcrowding.[11] Chicago's earliest gangs are also tied to European immigrant groups in the 1800s. Black gangs like Gangster Disciples or Vice Lords and Latino gangs like Latin Kings or Spanish Lords didn't emerge until the 1950s and 1960s.

On the West Coast, gangs are closely linked to Los Angeles in the early 1900s and have roots in Mexican communities. The origins connect to two major events: the Mexican Government ceding much of the West Coast land to the United States—leaving Mexican residents living on that land feeling marginalized and displaced by the newfound territory—and the Mexican Revolution, which caused an immigration wave to the U.S., where young men "coalesced under urban pressures."[11] The initial headlines associating Mexicans with gangs involved the Zoot-Suit Riots, where White off-duty sailors attacked Mexicans and stripped them naked of their Pachuco-style clothing.[12] Following these riots, Latino youth began organizing out of protection. Other Latino groups can be traced to car clubs and Civil Rights organizations such as the Brown Berets (inspired by the Black Panther Party). But the criminal street gangs were formed under prison gang umbrellas such as La Eme that united small barrio gangs, with the exception of independent gangs like El Hoya Maravilla. Other Latino gangs, ones with heritage from Central America, where people were also escaping civil unrest, began spawning as a resistance movement against the dominance of Mexican gangs. These included MS-13 or 18th Street.

Black clubs in LA can be traced to as early as the 1920s with sets such as the Gladiators, Businessman, Slausons, and other Black social clubs and car clubs. Many of these club members began joining the Civil Rights movement in the 1960s. These clubs later began morphing into criminal street gangs as a result of poverty, unemployment, and the racist dismantling of the Civil Rights movement. This led many Black youth away from positive social movements and into the lanes of criminal street gangs.[11] Broader disorganization of social systems can be linked to the formation of gangs for every racial identity. The stark difference between the earlier Black clubs to the contemporary criminal street gangs was the shift to where crime became a lifestyle and the driving factor for forming the group. The Crips were the first Black gang in LA to gain prominence, formed after the decline of the Black Panther Party. Initially created as a protection group, they later morphed into a drug and gun trafficking entity driven by violence and territorial claims. The Bloods arose later, uniting other gangs that didn't want to join the Crips, largely as a response to the Crips' growing dominance.

There are lots of different gangs in Long Beach, but the ones I mostly heard about growing up were the Crips, the Longos, and the Asian Boyz.

The local gang claiming the neighborhood I grew up in was the Longos. They're a Latino gang based in Long Beach under the Sureños, which represents the street soldiers of Southern California under the Mexican Mafia (La Eme) prison gang. The Eastside Longos claim an area east of the 710 freeway, and they are the largest faction of the Longos. Their strongest *cliqa* resides in the Washington Neighborhood: Barrio Viejo.

The history of this gang is fairly recent, starting around the 1960s. Izzy and I knew where this gang would hang out in the neighborhood because they would chase us on our walks home. That's when we would book it and turn on our basketball wheels. I did notice that I was only chased when

I was with my friends, who were mostly Black. It reminded me how gang violence often dips into racial animosity.

Long Beach is a well-known city of Crips. Snoop Dogg often proudly represents the gang on TV, with the Super Bowl halftime show where he threw up the Crip sign being one example. But a great number of young men have died due to criminal street gangs, so I don't think it's something to glorify. The artist Vince Staples does a better job of critiquing gang life rather than glamorizing it. In an interview, he bluntly calls gang life "stupid."

The major Crip factions in Long Beach are Rollin' 20s, Rollin' 80s, and the Insane Crips. On the east end of the Washington Neighborhood, members of Insane Crips are known for hanging out in that area. But the basketball court was often an intermediary space where members of the Longos and Crips would get some games in.

Some of the Asian gangs in Long Beach are the Asian Boyz and Tiny Rascal Gang, which formed in the 1980s as a way for Cambodian youth to protect themselves from the East Side Longos. After the Khmer Rouge genocide, Cambodian refugees came to Central Long Beach, making it the largest population of Cambodians outside of Cambodia. Many Asian gangs emulate styles of Black gangs, and some are in allegiance with the Crips.

There are lots of other gangs in Long Beach, including the Sons of Samoa on the Westside, but these were just a few that caused harm to the neighborhood I grew up in.

With the origins of these gangs in the neighborhood, I can trace their roots back to around a hundred years. It isn't that far back. They aren't permanent, as the park supervisor tried to argue. They were constructed under societal constraints.

Criminal street gangs aren't universal. They aren't a law of nature, bound by some unbreakable physics. They aren't a divine force. They haven't always been around like the trees and plants around us. They're a counterculture that humans created, operating within a larger social construct. Yes, the need to form tribes for advancement and protection is in human nature. This need for belonging and community is fundamental to humans, similar to a wolf pack or lion pride.

But the modern, organized violence part is not.

Criminal street gangs were formed as a subculture for communities that were denied opportunities for advancement, growth, and prosperity and instead had to endure racism, oppression, violence, social disorganization, and isolation. Gangs were a way to build community and walk with strength in numbers. Unfortunately, this natural human need to build community and protection ultimately backfired. Black, Brown, and Asian gangs went to war with each other. Many gangs in Long Beach exist because they had to protect themselves from the nearby gangs in the area. Gang violence was a symptom of unhealthy neighborhoods and inequities from communities of color being treated like lower-class humans. Its inception wasn't that long ago, which means *we can reverse it.*

How to reverse it has been something constantly on my mind. I have talked to aspiring gang members, former gang members, community interventionist workers, public servants, parents, and community leaders. One piece that everyone points to is young people's free time.

How are we engaging young people to devote their idle time to a path that's more appealing than gang life? How do we recruit them better than the big homies?

I've broken down all the potential engagement mediums that we can use to encourage youth to live a life of contribution...not carnage.

Engagement Mediums

Build an oasis of positive youth development that offers a cornucopia of mediums.

1. Sports (basketball, football, soccer, baseball, skateboarding, surfing, tennis, etc.)
2. Music (rapping, singing, poetry, producing, playing an instrument, joining a band)
3. Art (painting, acting, writing, videography, photography, performing)
4. STEM (science, technology, engineering, math, research, gaming)
5. Entrepreneurship (business, branding, startups, inventing)
6. Civics (debate, community service, activism, organizing, governance)

Sports bring that same camaraderie, brotherhood/sisterhood, prestige, and recognition that gangs do. It's also a safe space to release emotions through structured forms of aggressive play. Sports teams are a positive form of gangs that also emphasize belonging. They even have territorial claims in sports; teams are putting on for their school, representing their side of town. The boasting of strength just isn't centered around violence. It's around the prosocial development of athletic prowess that holds space for battle. Athletes often get passes from gangs. This route is one of the strongest deterrents to gang life, and gang members themselves often had sports dreams.

Music offers an outlet to release emotions and shed light on issues in the neighborhood. It's a powerful form of expression where people share childhood traumas, love stories, and the memories of their community. People often listen to music to navigate life obstacles. Providing space for studios, instruments, lessons, and places to form music groups can nurture your next singer/songwriter rather than a shot-caller.

Art comes in many forms of creative, mystical expression where you can tell a story about the life you live and the one you dream of—digital (videography, photography), physical (painting, drawing, writing, graffiti, sculpting), and theatrical (acting, performing). Art is multifaceted and promotes creativity in areas that often feel bleak or hopeless. This medium has shaped our world, from the design of our buildings to the clothes we wear. Graffiti is a form of expression often associated with street gangs and sometimes a precursor to gang violence. There is a way to harness that artistry through prosocial incubators that allow those artists to showcase their work in a meaningful way.

STEM is an underrated one. It allows you to explain the mechanisms of the world through science and math and build ecosystems through technology and engineering. There might be a mathematician in that local gang or the next Neil deGrasse Tyson. Bringing the world of technology and innovation to gang-involved youth can inspire them to make a positive impact on the world. It also ensures that those youth ride the wave of technological advancements rather than get left behind by communities in more affluent areas.

Entrepreneurship involves starting your own clothing line or coming up with a new business idea that solves an everyday problem. Fostering a culture of entrepreneurship can develop the mindset of a self-starter and business owner. It's harder to choose gang life when opportunities are plentiful and culturally affirming. In today's globalized digital world, there's a market for everything. The nonprofit Hidden Genius Project is already doing this one at a high level.

Civics can build that good-neighbor vibe and remind young people of their agency to make the world into what it should be. It entails people who speak up for the issues in their community and organize others to do the same. Civic engagement can range from urging your city to install more trash cans on your block to advocating for gun violence prevention on a national level. It also weaves into other domains. Musicians can play a song in support of a movement. A sports team can play for a cause, something the NBA is known for. Artists can make abandoned walls their canvas for a political message. Scientists can gather evidence on what direction we should move forward as a species. And entrepreneurs can build incubators of social development.

Engagement domains provide an outlet for youth, but they don't address the overarching identity of the community.

Collective Efficacy

A concept I obsessed over in college was *Collective Efficacy*: the willingness of neighbors to stand together to create a vibrant community. There's a strong connection between collective efficacy and neighborhood safety. Do residents watch over each other's homes and kids? Do residents come together to solve problems?

The backbone of collective efficacy is social cohesion. The more connected residents are to each other and their community, the more likely they are to step in when *the going gets tough*. This means calling the police when someone's house is being burglarized or watching out for the neighborhood kids. This could even mean mobilizing side by side at a City Council meeting to raise awareness about a dangerous intersection. Collective efficacy keeps neighborhoods safe.[13]

United neighborhoods don't let violence chew them up.

In a study by Brian R. Higgins and Joel Hunt, eight different neighborhoods were reviewed to determine what led to rises and falls in collective efficacy and social cohesion. One finding was that in neighborhoods with better-maintained public spaces, residents were more likely to protect their communities. The state of the environment contributed to a resident's decision to look out for their neighbors.

I saw this firsthand once in the more affluent area of Lakewood. My boy Izzy did his usual move—tossing his empty Hot Fries bag over his shoulder, aiming for the imaginary trash can that was the sidewalk. But this was different. Right after he tossed it, he hesitated and said, "Hold on, this Lakewood, I can't be doing that." He turned around, picked up the bag, and threw it away in a nearby trash can.

I giggled at the change in behavior; it didn't register with me at the time, but years later, it made me think. *He knew how well-kept the streets of Lakewood were, and he didn't want to mess with it.* But in his own neighborhood, which he saw trashed and littered, he was more than willing to treat it the same and continue the cycle. We unconsciously follow the pattern. It's time to take care of our public spaces and be mindful of the cycles we trip up on.

The dichotomy of my neighborhood compared to other parts of the city, or to Lakewood, gave fire to the mission. Many people can relate to this. You don't realize how fucked up your neighborhood is until you see how nice another one is. It's like when you realize your Christmas gift wasn't all that after hearing what your friend got. You're in this bubble of underinvestment and only break free once you peek over the fence where the grass is greener. This comparison brandishes a sword of energy for doing whatever you can to chop down that fence.

Those fences didn't get there by accident. No one puts up a fence and then says, "Oh my fault, I didn't know this was going to keep you out." The purpose was well-intended. My job was to break down the fence.

Collective efficacy does more than just prevent the neighborhood kid from tossing their chips bag on the floor. It can bring people together to prevent violence.

The idea of the *neighborhood kid* is rooted in collective efficacy. A neighborhood kid understands their agency to shape the environment around them. They have pride, resilience, and *deep awareness* and affection over the community that raised them. They want to look after it. Protect it. Build it up rather than tear it down. It took me a while to understand this concept of the neighborhood kid. One of the things that helped me realize this was basketball.

The game changed my life. It brought joy to a neighborhood overflowing with heartbreak. It gave me an outlet to express my frustrations and build community.

Basketball inspired hope for a better neighborhood.

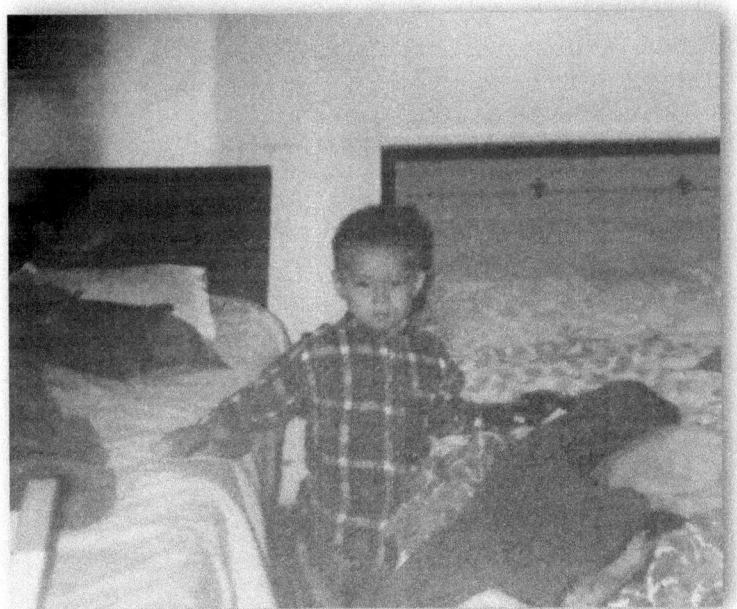

(My sandbox years rocking a fresh flannel—a staple of Chicano culture)

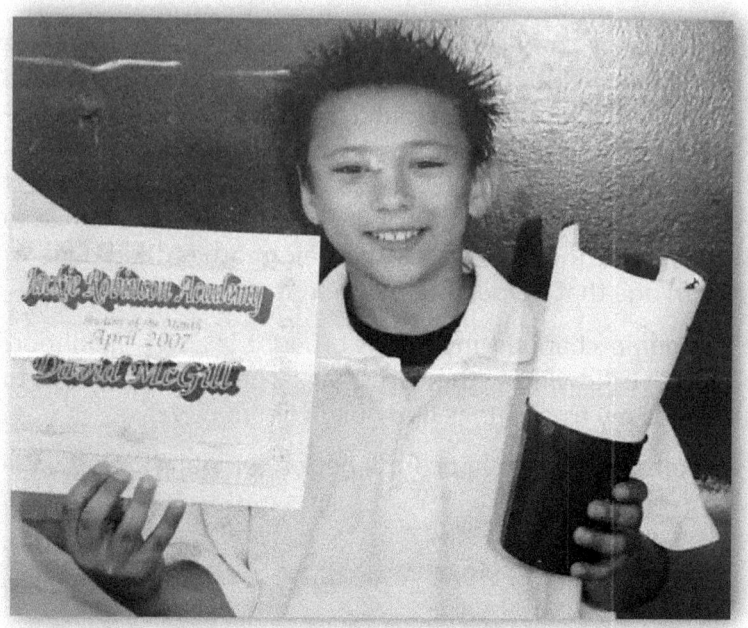

(My Student of the Month award just to prove a point)

(An everyday photo of territorial claims of street gangs in front of 14th Street Park—Jan 2025)

CHAPTER 3
NEIGHBORHOOD HOOPS

During my grade school years, I spent most of my free time with a basketball in hand. When I tried out for the basketball team at Jackie Robinson Academy in 7th grade, I didn't make the cut. That devastated me. And I took it personal.

That entire summer, I locked in, training relentlessly at the local 14th Street courts, in the back of my apartment, and at my dad's with the hoop he bought me. I had vengeance in sight. I came back in my 8th-grade year and not only made the team but was also named MVP. *Got 'em.*

The Courts

I grew up playing at the 14th Street courts in the Washington Neighborhood during primetime days, where even people from rival gangs would set their beef aside for some good runs. At least most of the time.

There was a time in 2013 when a gang member pulled up to the courts to confront a rival enemy. He brought a gun and just started shooting, even at those who weren't in a gang. Players scattered in different directions. Thankfully, no one was injured.

After that, the police department stationed a SWAT truck right in front of the courts off Locust Avenue for the next couple of weeks. Maybe as a deterrent. Maybe as surveillance. Either way, it was a reminder. Seeing that truck every day was a constant reminder of the danger around us. Basketball couldn't mask that.

As a neighborhood kid, I spent entire summer days at those courts. And gang violence wasn't the only heat on the block.

Those concrete floors would get blazing hot at the peak of summer, where you could feel the heat of the ground at the bottom of your shoes. You had to move around fast, push off the ground for every jump and run, to limit the time those soles remained kissed to the pavement. The Washington Neighborhood is one of the hottest neighborhoods in Long Beach, classified as an urban heat island.[14] A combination of limited green space, lack of trees, a concrete jungle of buildings, roads, and parking lots, the density of cars, and proximity to diesel trucks, refineries, and the idle port ships all contributed to the heat on the block. It was the first neighborhood selected for the Cooling Long Beach campaign to develop solutions to cool it down. But you didn't need a report to tell you how hot it was. You can see the heat in the neighborhood, full of potentially heat-induced frustrations, anger, and violence.

Our 14th Street courts had no bathroom, no trustworthy water fountain, and no place to sit because the bleachers were full of people living on them, so the City removed them. We were short on amenities but high on vulnerabilities. In terms of Environmental Impact scores that measure proximity to hazards, exposure to air pollution, and social health vulnerabilities, the Washington Neighborhood has one of the worst scores in all of LA County, which is the most populated county in the country and includes Los Angeles, Compton, and 85 other cities.[5]

The courts underwent several iterations of transformation. I remember when it was just two half courts with broken-up concrete and plastic nets. Those were the days when you had to watch where you dribbled or else it'd bounce off one of the cracks and you'd lose control. In 2011, they remodeled the courts, which brought out more players and gave the space new life.[15]

I learned a lot on those courts.

Once, during a five-on-five full-court game, I was shooting around on the opposite end of the court while waiting my turn. You were able to get some shots up on that side, but you had to scramble out of the way once they ran back. This particular time, I didn't get out of the way fast enough.

An OG—swole, built like a locomotive and Deebo hybrid—ran me over. I went flying, skidding across the concrete floor like my back was a snowboard. He screamed at me, "See, that's why you gotta get the hell out the way, lil' mothafucka!" He was well respected and a known Crip from the neighborhood. I didn't say a word, just grateful he didn't do anything else to me.

Izzy came over to console his fallen comrade, "Yo, that ain't right what he did. You good?" as he tapped my chest with the back of his palm as if to cheer me up. "Yeah, I'm good," responding with a tone of grit as I got up and shook Izzy's hand to reinforce the statement and snap out of the mental spiral that kept replaying what just went down. I discreetly wiped the concrete shavings off my body, double-checked the grip on my shoes as if lack of traction was to blame, and waited to play next in the green-linked fenced corner, carrying the ball as it rested on my hip.

That moment made me tough. I didn't let the ego hit of being knocked down to the ground in front of everyone get to me. I stood strong, head held high, played next with a chip on my shoulder, and won the game. It was a lesson in resilience, emotional intelligence, and self-control, things you must learn to survive in a neighborhood that is constantly testing you.

Neighborhood Medium

Basketball was our medium: a mode of transportation to a life that didn't involve gangs, drugs, smoking, alcohol, and violence. We saw it as a bridge, a way out. I have no idea what we would've done without those courts in the neighborhood. Basketball is just one medium or bridge that guides young people toward a life of sustenance. Being an athlete was often a pass for a gang to leave us alone.

One day, Izzy and I were playing at a mobile park from the Parks & Rec Department. They had a portable basketball court set up from a storage truck right there on 16th Street and Pine. We played a game of 21 that day with an older Black dude who pretty much dominated us. Right before he left, he asked, "Do y'all bang?"

"Na, we don't bang," we answered while in fear that something might pop off.

"Ahh, alright, stay outta gangs, but if you do want to join a gang, make sure to join my gang," he said as he walked away with an extra oomph in his step from the beat down he gave us.

He respected our devotion to basketball, as if he wished he could focus on the sport too but that it was too late for him. Basketball scooped us up in time. Mediums of all sorts present themselves as better options than gang violence.

These bridges change lives and keep neighborhoods safe. Of course, it's hard to pledge your focus to these mediums if your basic needs aren't met first.

The PCLs

I was 10 years old when my mom finally found stable housing. A brand-new affordable housing complex called Pacific City Lights had opened up in the Washington Neighborhood off Pacific and 16th.[16] Our neighbor Antagracia encouraged my mom to apply, but she hesitated at first. When you're undocumented, it's hard to trust all that paperwork stuff. You don't want to submit all of the information out of fear that they will release it to law enforcement and try to deport you. Still, she played her cards, took the risk, and applied anyway. She prayed every night with my sisters and me, kneeling by the bed. Mom went through all the interviews held at the complex. I remember thinking, "Wow, this place is nice. If we lived here, life would be so much better."

In the end, we secured a spot as one of the first families to move in. Antagracia applied, too, but didn't get in. The family who encouraged us didn't even get accepted. We got lucky, and to this day, we're grateful Antagracia pushed my mom to apply.

When we moved in, my sisters and I made our mom promise we'd stay longer than a year. We were moving every year for over five years in a row and were tired of the instability. Mom promised us at least five years and fulfilled it. The stability of living there with an affordable rent payment adjusted to my mom's income changed our lives. The place was nice and spacious with two bathrooms and three bedrooms, a big upgrade from the one-bedroom, one-bathroom situation we were used to. Technically, it was low-income housing, but it didn't look like the projects. It felt like it, though. Everyone navigated the same social obstacles as we did: poverty, violence, and disinvestment.

We called it the PCLs. It's where I met Izzy, Vincent, Samuel, Eric, T.O., Lil' Frank, Big Frank, Roger, Mike, and so many other neighborhood kids who benefited from affordable housing. Our days were spent in the back of the apartments, doing everything from wrestling, rapping, and dancing (we even had a jerking crew for a bit) to playing football and basketball, clowning around, or just chopping it up. We even had a computer lab run by the nonprofit, Centro CHA. The lab was led by a young man named Francisco, who was just doing his best. We gave him a hard time, as we were some meddling kids for sure.

I made so many childhood friends at those apartments, but none of my friendships were stronger than the bond Izzy and I had. We did everything together. We became skateboarders, ding-dong ditchers, basketball players, dancers, and anything that fit our imagination. He was my partner in crime, figuratively and literally. We'd steal, break windows, hop fences, and do anything else young boys do with too much free time. I remember we used to take our skateboards to the top of the hill near Washington Middle School, sit on them, and then ride through the street, allowing momentum to take us up a couple of blocks.

Izzy was the best ding-dong ditcher in the apartment. He was fearless, or maybe just addicted to the adrenaline of running away. Once, he banged on the same door within an hour. I guess he felt one wave wasn't enough. During this second time, the mom must've been waiting by the door. Because as soon as he started knocking on the metal door, the mom immediately opened it, grabbed Izzy, and yanked him into her home. Izzy started screaming, placing his hands out to grab onto the spine of the doorway. It looked like a scene from a scary movie.

And when we weren't messing around in the apartment building, we were walking to Eddie's Liquor down the street. Izzy and I would each have $1 that we collected from asking neighbors for donations to some made-up program we were in. We would buy a Honey Bun and a Shasta soda. Each was 50 cents, so it turned into a meal for us. The Shasta and Honeybun would be gone before we made it back home, so we didn't have to give it all away to the kids feening for some. If you gave someone a waterfall, it'd turn into an empty can.

That was a legendary neighborhood snack. It wasn't good for us by any means, but it was what we could afford, and we were grateful for it. Those were some green lights in the neighborhood, man.[17]

Not everything was a highlight, though. I noticed that my neighborhood was a desert of youth programs, hardly any around. All we had to get better at basketball was the busted-up portable And1 hoop in our apartment or our beloved 14th Street courts. It wasn't structured. I realized it wasn't enough when we made it to high school and weren't as good as everyone else. The small middle school environment kept us in a bubble once we arrived at a 3,200+ student body high school. We learned that people were playing travel ball while we were just playing street ball. I almost didn't even play basketball in high school.

I went to Cabrillo High School on the Westside of Long Beach and nervously tried out for the basketball team. Hardly any Latinos were trying out, even though the student body was majority Latino. They had two days of tryouts, and on the first day, they didn't call my name. They did call Izzy's name. He was fairly tall, had long arms, and was athletic, rocking the Allen Iverson braids. That was an easy choice. But the shorter kid with spiky hair and shorter arms didn't really look like a hooper.

That night, I went to the 14th Street courts to train and get better before the final day. I ended up tearing a ligament in one of the fingers on my shooting hand during a random game of 21. I took a few weeks off to recover, and I thought my playing days were done. Ironically, I was a bit relieved because now I had an excuse as to why I didn't make the team.

Thankfully, *my mom wasn't having it.*

Mom Saved the Game

My mom didn't give a fuck. She was going to get her son another shot at the basketball team. I also think she felt a sense of mission to help get a Mexican student on the basketball team, something you didn't see that often.

She took me with her on a march up to the practices of the newly selected squads. She had to speak with the program's head coach, Coach Jay. He was a 6'8", former college standout athlete who could've gone pro. He had this powerful, respect-demanding voice. My mom is about two feet shorter than he is, literally. But it didn't matter. She went up there to tell Coach Jay to give her son one more shot at making the team. I watched them go back and forth as I waited at a nearby court, shooting around by myself. He towered over her in physicality, but her determination stood even taller. After a while of deliberation, my mom walked away, and Coach Jay called me over. "Dave, gonna give you one more shot at making this team, man. I heard you missed the end of tryouts because you hurt your hand. Well, now let's see what you got. Don't let me down." He sent me over to the sophomore team to play a one-on-one drill called King of the Court. As much as my mom would've wanted to hop on that court with me to make sure we dunked on the other players, there wasn't anything else she could do. The ball was in my court.

I got my rhythm going after I made a stop on defense. I had the ball with the next defender lined up. The defender throws you the ball and then runs up to lock you down. They were thinking, "Who is this random, short, spiky-haired kid jumping into our practice session tryin' to take my spot?" Right after the defender threw the ball, I launched it from downtown at the three-point line. *Bang*. Knocked it down. The next defender grabs the change. He throws the ball while running up to me a bit slower, thinking I wasn't going to shoot again. I threw that thing up like there was no tomorrow. *Bang Bang*. Cashed the second three-pointer in a row. Too easy.

Coach Jay saw me knock them both down and said "Okay Daaaaaave, I see you." That was it. I made the team. There was no looking back.

Izzy and I held our own that first year with the help of our street toughness, but we were far from the best. I came off the bench, averaging two three-pointers a game. As a result, I worked out all summer long at 14th Street courts and a YMCA gym across town. My sister Denise, my mom, and my Dad gave me rides whenever they could, or I'd hop on the bus. Those days could go from 6 am to 5 pm, multiple workouts throughout the day, getting up shots until my legs gave in. I remember hardly having any money to buy food while out and about. When I would train with Izzy, we would unite our money to buy cheap bread from a grocery store to keep us full or peruse the dollar menu at a fast food joint.

I thought if I just worked hard that I would be great.

I returned the second year with Coach Jay respecting my game due to being one of the best shooters in the school. He also respected my work ethic and gave me an easy path to junior varsity, even though over 100 people tried out. I was in the starting lineup on that team for a few games, but we were horrible. I was, too. We went unwinnable 0-11, even losing to sum really bad team from Compton. I remember one of their players had Vans on and was giving us buckets. We laughed at how bad we were. I couldn't figure out why my game stayed the same, if not worsened, despite training all summer. I wanted to be great, but the results of my efforts had little returns.

Lakewood Hoops

I remember running into the President of Lakewood Hoops while working out at the YMCA one day. Lakewood Hoops was a sports-based development enterprise that turned out college and pro-level athletes, including NBA player Landry Fields. They trained big time talent for an hourly rate. At the time, I blew it off because I couldn't afford it, and my mom and I agreed that I could train myself. I'd watch their training sessions at the YMCA and copied their drills. But after an underperforming sophomore year season, I knew I needed something more. I couldn't afford a travel ball team and wasn't good enough for a team to sponsor me. I couldn't afford joining this program either. I didn't have many options going for me. Then I remembered that when the President encouraged me to join, I told him I couldn't afford it, and he responded with "Don't worry about all that." He was telling me not to worry about the money and just join and pay whatever I could. So I pulled out the business card he gave me and called him up the summer leading into my junior year. He told me to come out to Del Valle Park in Lakewood. I was leaving my neighborhood to join this youth program. It was over an hour bus ride on the Long Beach Transit 172 bus from Pacific and 16th across town to Palo Verde and Del Amo. After you got off the bus, you still had a 20-minute walk to the park. It was a trek, but I was pursuing my dream of *making it in basketball so that I could make it out of the neighborhood.*

That bus ride out of the neighborhood was a turning point in my life. It changed my life. My world.

The program was *built different*. The drills were innovative, and having someone push me brought out my best. The Lakewood Hoops program had me training with some of the top high school players in the region and even college-level athletes, including Jordan Bell from Oregon, who went on to win an NBA championship. The lineup at this basic outdoor court in the blistering sun was crazy. Big-time talent like that you only see in fancy gyms with air conditioning. It showed how much credibility Lakewood Hoops had in the hooper circles. I remember lining up for drills: in front of me was Professor, a hooper going to Cal Poly; behind me was Pepe, who became an overseas pro; and behind him was Tyler Harvey, who ended up getting drafted to the NBA, to name a few. Once, I played one-on-one full-court with an overseas pro named Patrick Rembert. I took a major L, but I learned so much from going head-to-head with him. My social circle changed again. I started living and breathing basketball on a whole new level.

At the same time, though, I was a mediocre academic student. I acted like a clown in school and was barely passing with Cs, thanks to the girls who helped me with all my work. But the President of Lakewood Hoops inspired me to shape up. He motivated me to get straight A's.

One day, after a rough training session, he asked me, "How them grades doing." I told him, "I got a couple Cs, a B, one D," throwin' in an excuse about the teacher or sum. He responded with emotion: "That's not going to cut it. We get A's around here. Everyone gets A's over here. Jacob (who was my age and the best kid in the program) gets straight As. You get *no looks without the books.*" He repeated. "I need straight As. You do your best in everything you do, not just on the basketball court." That was all I needed. It lit flames in my stomach. I started grinding in the classroom just as hard as I would on the court. I started to take my academics as seriously as the game. I no longer saw it as separate. They were related—integrated, interconnected, and intertwined into the fabric of my ticket out. My grades were going to help me play college basketball. *You get no looks without the books.* I obsessively replayed it in my head.

Dad's Financial Battles

That speech wasn't the only thing that made me turn it around in the classroom. Around the same time I joined Lakewood Hoops, my dad and I got evicted from our home. Money and Dad never got along. They would square up with each other, with Money usually getting Dad in a headlock. He couldn't budget to save his life. Even after going from a low-paying security guard to a decent teaching salary, money problems still haunted us. Dad would often remind me, "Money's tight right now, son," when I would ask for something. That era of "money being tight" never ended.

I remember getting so frustrated at my dad after he gave the same repetitive excuse about how he couldn't afford something I really wanted that, in a spill of anger and sadness while crying my eyes out, I yelled, "Why don't you just go to the ATM and pull out money? ATMs are everywhere. It's easy!" as my arms stretched out, palms up in exhaustion. He took a long pause with a sigh of regret while looking out into the distance as he searched for an answer to quell my clueless mind. "It's not that easy, son."

I remembered that "It's not that easy" line so vividly. I replayed it in my head once I learned why you can't just pull out money from ATMs whenever you want.

Buying new uniforms was financial warfare. My mom and dad passed me around back and forth like a hot potato, disagreeing about who should buy me what. I'd ask my mom for new uniforms, and she'd tell me to ask my dad. Then I'd ask him, and he'd say he couldn't afford them because money was tight, encouraging me to ask my mom to buy them. I gave up on asking and squeezed into my overgrown, beat-up uniform.

At one point, I only had one pair of shorts I liked wearing, and that looked good on me. I think I miscalculated how much I could get away with wearing them because I made the mistake of wearing those shorts every day for one week in 5th grade. The kids don't miss nothing.*

I was minding my own business while standing in line on the blacktop painted lines in front of the handball wall, waiting for our teacher to bring us back to class. A classmate, Camila—whom I think liked me—called me out. "Haha, that's why you wear the same shorts every day. With yo dirty, stinky butt."

I was silent, quivering in shame. I had no comeback. She got me good. I put the tease in my back pocket to save for later because I knew that one day, I could buy my own clothes.

The lowest point in my Dad's money struggles was when we wanted to go out to eat dinner at Hometown Buffet. That was our spot because we could eat two or three meals in one sitting. Dad didn't have money for it that particular evening, but he did have an old sauce jar full of pennies, nickels, dimes, and quarters. We rolled it out and started counting, using our index fingers to group out the coins and scrape out as many silver ones as possible to avoid the hundred-pennies-per-dollar nightmare. Paying for our meals with a whole bunch of coins in front of a line of people staring at us was never a proud moment. These financial problems eventually led to us being kicked out of our apartment.

It was a long day of school and practice when we got home at our duplex spot. This was the most stable place my Dad ever rented. He had just started teaching at Dominguez High, finally earning a steady income after years of substitute gigs and security guard shifts. It was a solid place. He had put up a basketball court in the driveway where I would spend hours playing him one-on-one, doing shooting drills, and imitating the Kobe fadeaway until I mastered it. Those one-on-one games would get intense, often ending in laughter and our dog barking out of excitement.

On this particular evening, we were arriving home after a long school and work day, excited about our spaghetti night for dinner.

As we walked up to the blue-painted porch, we let Snugs out of his side yard, and he made his usual attempt to jump straight up on the porch from the tall side of it rather than going around to the steps. Snugs was our little dachshund mixed with some beagle, and maybe a lil wolf, who I loved so much. What wasn't usual was this pinkish piece of paper that was left at the door in between the metal bars of the screen. My Dad snatched it as if he didn't want me to see it. You could see the emotions on his face after reading it: His eyes were tilted low, and his lips curled in a gesture of surrender, finished with a sigh of helplessness. There was an awkward silence. I wasn't sure what it was. I asked him, and he almost reluctantly said in a somber tone, "It's an eviction notice. They are telling us we have to leave. We can't live here anymore," as he turned the key and opened the door.

I entered our home in a state of confusion. Walking through the living room, but mostly just thinking. I had no idea it was coming. Within a matter of days, we had to go. All the normalcy we had just created in that place was stripped away. There were so many memories left behind.

My dad moved in with his mom for a while and then transitioned into renting a room in different places around town. My option was to move in with my grandma, too, but instead, I opted to live with my mom 100% since I was going back and forth to each place for years.

That moment reminded me how fragile your housing situation can be. How fragile stability could be. It flipped a switch in me. I locked in like never before.

Education was my pathway out of this life of instability. My bridge. I decided that money would no longer be a problem for me in the future. Education would be my bridge out of poverty. I didn't know exactly how it would serve that purpose. But I always felt that if I did my best in basketball and education, *everything else would fall into place.*

Hoop Dreams

The inspiration from Lakewood Hoops and getting evicted put me in a completely different mindset than some of my boys from the PCLs. During my first year of high school, Izzy was one of my only friends. We did everything together. But we stopped hanging out due to a few conflicts on and off the court. So instead, I started hanging out with the varsity basketball players, hoping to be accepted. Tall dudes with flattops and bounce. I wanted to be on their team.

You choose your social circles based on where you want to be in life. If you want to be an engineer, hang out with a bunch of engineers, or join an online community if you don't know any. If you want to be a founder of an innovative company, find examples of founders who have started great companies and reach out to them. Or at least absorb everything they put out and learn from them from afar. I just wanted to be on the varsity team, so what better step than spending my free time around them? I was slowly becoming who I wanted to be. My surroundings weren't the only thing changing either—my game was too.

You choose your social circles based on where you want to be in life.

The Lakewood Hoops program turned me into a completely different player that summer before my junior year. I started dominating and taking charge. When my junior year began, I knew it would be different. I was moved up to the varsity team and became a starter. In my first home game, I dropped 17 points against Wilson High School. I hit a deep NBA-range three that no one expected me to make during one of the crunch-time moments of the game. I had the crowd in it, and we kept it close until the end. We lost the game, but I won the respect of my peers. That night, everyone in the stands was like, "Where did this dude come from?" He came out of nowhere." Someone even chased me down and asked for my autograph. That wasn't just a breakout game. There was a hidden purpose to it.

I honored that game to my dog, Snugs. He wasn't just a dog; he was my son, my best friend.

Snugs was a daredevil. He had this fearless habit of tippy-toeing on my knee while I was sitting in the passenger seat of my dad's SUV, just to peek his head out the window. On one occasion, as my Dad drove down an on-ramp of a major freeway, he accelerated, unaware of the red light ahead. I quickly pointed it out and urged him to shift to the carpool lane so we didn't have to stop. After it registered with him, Dad pounded the brakes so he could change lanes before he ran the red.

Upon smashing the brake pedal with my Dad's heavy foot, Snugs just teleports. *Pooof.* He was gone in a split second. From his two little paws on my right knee and head over the rearview mirror, to completely gone with the wind. The sudden brake check caused Snugs to fling out the window and into the abyss of the freeway. Myself, my Dad, and my friend in the back, all screamed our lungs out: "Oh fuck!" or "Ahhhhh!" or "Snugggss!" all at once. I don't know who said what. We were so loud that the voices just blended into one.

My Dad pulls over to the side, hoping Snugs is alive back there. He quickly jumps out, car still running. I plop up on my knees and turn around in my seat to see what's going on. I see our little dog walking around the freeway onramp in a daze. His eyes revealed confusion, not knowing what just happened or where he's at. My Dad scoops him up like a bird with a broken wing. He runs back before any cars come and gently puts Snugs back on my lap. There were street burns all over him from head to toe. From the look of the wounds, he tried to catch his balance after landing, but tumbled from the momentum.

Snugs was fine. It took him a while to trust the window again, and we learned our lesson.

But a few years later, we had to give Snugs back to the pound. I last saw him on January 5, 2014. His back legs gave out, resulting in digestive problems and back spasms. He would crawl around using his two front paws while his back legs dragged, lifeless. Before that, Snugs was a big-time jumper, clearing several flights of stairs, jumping onto tall beds, and even into my dad's SUV. Snugs would get so excited when we let him roam outside that instead of using the four stairs on the porch to go down, he would leap over them—with his legs straight out like Superman, while he glided in the air as if he sprang from a diving board. I think all that jumping did him in and paralyzed his back legs, a common issue for weiner dogs, given their long backs. We had to give him back to the pound where we picked him up several years earlier.

To honor Snugs, I put the date of the last day I saw him on my green Kobe 8s, which I wore for my first year of varsity basketball. Teammates would ask, "What's that on your shoes?" I didn't want them to make fun of me for honoring my dog, so I told them, "For someone in my family." It was the truth. That first game was for Snugs, no doubt about it.

Basketball's Life Lessons

I was excited about what my basketball career had in store. A few days after my first varsity home game, I went to Lakewood Hoops to put in more work. The President asked how my game went and how many points I had. I humbly responded as I walked onto the court, "It was a close one, but we lost in the end. I had 17."

"Daaaaaammn, you had 17, like that?" It was a welcome surprise to hear from someone who usually put up six points a game.

Looking back, basketball didn't directly get me out of poverty. I didn't make the NBA or play overseas. I said 17, not 40. I didn't become a big-time coach or trainer either. But basketball gave me the skillset to succeed at anything I do. It taught me that hard work makes a promise—a promise that some result will follow. *And hard work never breaks its promises.* That was the lesson of work ethic I learned from the game.

Hard work never breaks its promises.

Basketball also taught me teamwork. No matter how good you are, you need a solid team around you. Choose your circle wisely. *Your life will mimic the lives of those around you.* If you have a strong team in your corner, you're never alone in your endeavors.

Your life will mimic the lives of those around you.

Basketball even taught me leadership. My first venture into leadership was serving as the captain of the varsity team. I wasn't even the best player on the team, let alone the second-best. We had some big-time talent like my boys Sequan and Mike, who dropped 20 points a night like it was nothing. But I was the best leader. I set the tone by showing up early, staying late, and starting our drills without waiting on our coach. Leadership also means addressing conflict. I had to navigate the tension between players. Conflicts from teammates clashing or players vying for the same spot were moments that tested me. And that wisdom from experience has stayed with me ever since. Work ethic. Teamwork. Leadership. Basketball schooled me in all of them.

I'm not the only one who sees basketball as a teacher of life. Kobe Bryant himself has discussed this in multiple interviews.[18] The game taught him how to navigate obstacles, keep emotions leveled, and become hyper-focused on a single objective. I didn't know it then, but the most important life lessons I was gaining in high school weren't in a classroom. They were right there on that old, reliable basketball court.

During those last couple of years of high school, my social persona was crafted. I was on top of the world. Basketball was going great with the help of Lakewood Hoops. I was captain and president of basketball operations. I was getting straight A's in AP and Honors classes. My peers voted me Most Likely to Succeed. And I was dating the beautiful homecoming queen.

I was ready to take the next step. It was time to make it out of the neighborhood. *No more games.*

(The front of Pacific City Lights where Izzy and I grew up)

(Summer 2014—winning MVP in Lakewood Hoops)

(Fall 2015—my teammates and I hanging out on the side of the gym)

PART II

THE WORK OF THE NEIGHBORHOOD AND THE NEIGHBORHOOD KID

MADE IT OUT

My homies in the Washington Neighborhood weren't getting accepted into universities like I was. Many of them didn't even know how to apply. I foolishly saw this as a badge of honor, a leg up that set me apart. But I had no idea how hard it would be to leave them and my neighborhood behind.

Choose Chico

I was accepted into most of the schools I applied to, including UCLA. Only five students from Cabrillo High got into UCLA, and I was the only one who turned down the offer. People called me dumb, foolish, or questioned my judgment. And they might've been right.

I remember arguing with my sister about it. "You should go to UCLA. My mentor told me that having it on your resume would make getting a job a lot easier," she said.

I defensively shot back, "I want to play college basketball, and I know damn well I have no chance for that at UCLA."

She was just looking out for me. "But do you even know for sure if you'll play at Chico State?" she said.

"Oh, I'm going to play there. I know that for sure," I replied, banking on my drive and will to do whatever it took.

She was wholeheartedly concerned about my future, as any big sis would be. But my dream of basketball was greater than any prestige of a school. I didn't put in all that hard work in the classroom for the sake of school. I did it to go play college basketball somewhere. It was "no looks without the books." I only excelled in the books for the looks of college basketball scouts. That was my main dream.

Out of the six universities that accepted me, Chico State had the most potential for a college basketball opportunity, according to the Lakewood Hoops program and my high school head coach. Located in the small city of Chico, a 500-mile eight-hour drive from Long Beach that's full of grapevines and farms. A top 25 party school in the nation, but to me, it was a vessel en route to my dreams out of the neighborhood. My high school head coach said he knew the coaches there and could get me set up as a walk-on. "If you do what you need to do, you will be on the team as a redshirt freshman," he told me. So, I took the chance and committed to Chico State.

Going to Chico State was also a way to prove one of my assistant coaches wrong. One day at practice, my assistant coach sat me down to keep it real about my future. He was a shorter guy who loved to yell and kind of looked like a fish. "I see you as a Division III college basketball player," he said, trying to curb my expectations. I took it as an insult. It motivated me to go after a Division II or higher playing career to prove him wrong. I even had an opportunity to play at the Division III school, Whittier College, and at Long Beach City College, where the coach encouraged me to join his team. I passed up both options to prove myself as a Division II player somewhere far from the neighborhood.

I wanted to leave Long Beach, live in the dorms, and flex on the homies, "Yeah, I'm headed out to Chico State." It was a chance to demonstrate that basketball was my ticket out of the neighborhood's low educational attainment rates.

In my neighborhood, many people don't even have a high school diploma.

I had my ticket—a nonstop trip out of the hood. However, I had no idea what challenges lay ahead.

I had several "firsts" in Chico: first time living on my own, first time having sex, first time getting arrested. It was a hell of a splash into adulthood.

Chico was a whole different world from the schools and neighborhoods I was used to. It sat in the middle of nowhere, about 2 hours north of Sacramento. Chico was nothing like Long Beach—massive trees, middle-of-nowhere highways, and a surrounding edge that led to farms and mountains. Chico State's faculty and student body included people from more affluent areas like Petaluma and Napa—California's Wine Country.

I was so determined to go there that on my first visit, I took a 13-hour Greyhound bus ride. It was miserable sitting on that bus. They made countless stops. It stank. And as a 17-year-old neighborhood kid traveling alone for the first time, I was on edge the entire ride. The whole 26-hour round trip tested my resilience and endurance. My work ethic was on full display. I gave everything I had to embark on a new journey in uncharted waters.

Culture Shock

That neighborhood culture I was used to was no longer the top dawg. I felt it from day one.

With my fresh Pro Club, cargo pants, and chain on my neck, people knew I was from the hood from the way I dressed to the way I said things. Saying things like "funna go to the store," "good lookin' out," "conversating," or talking in a quick mumble were things they weren't used to. I hated feeling like the odd man out. I started second-guessing how I dressed and how I spoke. I wanted to fit in. So I started dressing like the boys there: a colorful tank top, jogger pants, and a visor hat. I was trying to blend in, chameleon style. I used less slang, tucked in my chain, and gave up on the Pro Clubs.

The culture shock hit even harder when basketball was taken from me. In my early weeks at Chico State, I met with the head coach and several assistants. My high school coach gave them a heads-up, so they already knew I was coming for a walk-on opportunity. I let them know who I was and what I wanted to bring to the team. We talked a bit, and they asked about my highlights and stats. Then they hit me with the hammer: I'd have to wait until the following year to try out because all the roster spots were full. That one hit hard. I thought they were going to give me a chance if "I did what I needed to do." Not a chance I had of getting on that Division II team, one of the best in the country.

I was foolish to think I could jump on the team. I trusted my high school coach a little too much. I shouldn't have let someone's word determine my life trajectory. You gotta have more evidence than that. Playing college basketball is so hard: Only about 3% of high school basketball players take their talents to the college level.[19]

Basketball was my sanctuary, my anchor that kept me grounded. I was thrown out of alignment when it was taken from me.

Be a Man

While navigating college dorm life without basketball as my safe haven, I also struggled with the idea of masculinity. Back in the neighborhood, young men prove their manhood through dominance. This precipitates much of the gang violence we see in the area. Beating someone up, robbing, shooting, and just sheer victimization were cues of manliness. I avoided that trap by proving my masculinity through sport. But when basketball was snatched from me, my sense of masculinity came into question.

In college, masculinity was measured by sexual prowess. The more girls you hooked up with, the more of a man you were. The most revered guys in the hallway of the dorms were the ones who brought home girls after every party. If you came back alone, they'd ask, "What happened?" like you failed some agreed-upon conquest.

At the time, I had never slept with a girl. Everyone assumed I had been with a girl before because I had a girlfriend back home. I ran with it and kept the truth to myself until I could change it. A few months into the college party life, I hooked up with a girl simply to avoid being exposed. It wasn't about intimacy or connection. It was about gaining approval from the men around me. I was afraid of the bros who would call some men "virgins," instead of their actual names, as a form of ridicule and reminder of their weakness. I gave in to the pressures and had casual sex devoid of feelings. I caved in and did what I was told men are supposed to do. *Being able to deflect peer pressure and people pleasing is a skill I wish I had back then.*

> **Being able to deflect peer pressure and people pleasing is a skill I wish I had back then.**

But the struggle of what it meant to be a man was the last of my worries at the time, honestly. Because for the first time in my young, spring life, my health was in question.

Acne Nightmare

I was out of my element—angry at the loss of basketball, around a lot of alcohol, smoking, drugs, reckless casual sex, eating only cookies and milk for dinner as if I was Santa Claus, hardly sleeping, and dealing with stressful encounters in the dorms. I kept it all repressed inside. I didn't talk to anyone about these battles. I didn't share it with my dad, mom, sisters, or close friends. I held it in.

Everything in my world was flipped upside down. It showed in my spirit, my health, and on my face.

It all happened in late 2015, over just a couple of months: I broke out with some serious, severe cystic acne like you've never seen. Acne came out in places it had never come out before. On my cheeks, back, shoulders, forehead, temples, neck, everywhere. I looked like I had a contagious disease and was turning into a zombie with big nodules all over me. Girls stopped giving me the time of day. People's eyelids would shoot up in disbelief when they saw my face. Everywhere I went, I got unsolicited advice: "Go all-natural," "Try this product," "I know a guy," or the worst one, "Damn, are you on drugs?"

It was one of the most difficult periods of my life. I remember breaking down on my dorm room bed while my roommate was away, out of frustration from not being able to figure it out. I tried various remedies, including creams, washes, masks, antibiotics, dietary changes, stress management, exercise, and sleep, but the issue persisted. It took years before I got it under control with prescription meds like Adapalene and Accutane. Some of the medications had their own side effect profiles and only masked the problem.

Years later, I realized my body was screaming at me, trying to tell me something. It was a warning that my life was out of alignment. Reduced physical activity, severe stressors from my living situation, the dining hall diet of cookies and cereal, internal battles of not belonging, anger from failing at my dream, hormonal imbalance, and even potential infection from an unsanitary environment were all accomplices. My body was trying to tell me that something was off, but instead of listening, I saw it as just another battle to fight.

All the battles coming my way after leaving the neighborhood were starting to stack up against me. *I was feeling outnumbered.*

But I made it out though, right? I was over 500 miles away, in some nice lil town with all these privileged kids. Everyone back home thought I was the man at Chico State, living the dream.

If it was a dream, it was one I wanted to wake up from.

I wasn't hooping, and my health was slipping. I went from being on top of everything the summer before college to hitting rock bottom with barely a social circle to lean on. I wanted to tap out. I wanted to come home. Make a return. But I couldn't. It would've meant coming home a failure. Dropping out.

After all the accolades? After all the hype?

Most Likely to Succeed, remember?
UCLA accepted, remember?
Chico State committed, remember?

What would it all be for then?

I just couldn't fathom dropping out. So, I went with the next best play—putting in for a transfer. But that meant grinding it out until the end of my sophomore year to rack up enough credits. I just had to keep my head down.

So with basketball out of the picture, I focused all my attention on my education.

Hollywood Cop

I chose to study Criminal Justice because I remembered the gang that burglarized my home in The Dales, and I wanted to figure out how to prevent that from happening to others.

I first got involved in law and justice in high school by joining a small learning community called Cal-J. It was full of students who wanted to be lawyers because they saw their families decimated by mass incarceration, or students who sold drugs and wanted to know how to stay a step ahead of the cops. That's where I officially started learning about law enforcement.

I grew up dreaming I'd become a big-time police officer, saving the day with guns blazing. Man, Hollywood puts a powerful trance on young people, shaping how they see their futures. You don't have many models of professionals who live in the neighborhood, so your biggest career aspirations are based on the big screen. Neighborhood kids have to bet their dreams on blockbuster movies and TV shows because the other options were gangs or low-paying, back-breaking jobs.

My professional career was in shotgun, and the destination was to become a cop. I joined the Criminal Justice Student Association, served as Vice President, organized FBI presentations, shot guns at the gun range, taught people how to shoot guns, toured prisons and juvenile halls, and organized K-9 officer demonstrations. I was all in, even with the mustache.

I landed a job as a Community Services Officer for the Chico State University Police Department, where I had everything an officer had—except a gun. Students called us rent-a-cops, wannabe cops, or mall cops. One of the funniest memories was when a student hollered at my partner, "Aye, you dropped your gun!" My partner looked at the ground behind her as if she was supposed to have a gun on her belt. Once she realized she didn't carry a gun, there was nothing to do but smile and shake your head. That was a good one.

But the teases didn't get to me. And there were perks, too, don't get me wrong. You would occasionally meet a girl who liked a man in uniform and called you cute. I also felt legit on that police radio, wearing my bulletproof vest, earpiece, and SWAT-style boots that made me a little over six feet tall—proudly responding when students pressed the emergency blue light late at night, requesting a safe ride home. I loved reporting things happening on campus. "This is UPD 53, we have a naked male running around the southwest parking lot of Sutter Hall." I even enjoyed yelling at people to get off their bikes.

One time, at a fire Mongolian BBQ spot, I was still wearing a law enforcement shirt when a mom with two kids came up to me and said, "Thank you for your service and everything you do to keep us safe."

It was starting to feel real.

I was in locker rooms with police officers, shooting the shit and shooting guns in my free time. In my mind, I was becoming that Hollywood cop.

Then, out of nowhere, I had a vision that put a serious dent in my plans.

Licienciado

In my criminal justice research methods class, while creating an e-portfolio, I was pasting a picture of New York police officers side by side. They all looked alike. I sat there in a trance, just thinking. I leaned back in my chair to let my mind go to work. *They all looked the same, en serio.* I couldn't see a difference. They stood as soldiers, ready to take orders. I thought to myself, *Do I want to be another soldier?* Was that why I joined this field? I wanted to have an impact on as many people as possible in my neighborhood and neighborhoods like it.

It didn't add up. Then it hit me.

It was an epiphany moment. You have those along the way and never know when they're coming. Right then and there, I decided I wasn't going to be a police officer. I wanted to think bigger.

As a police officer, my impact would be limited by the ranks in charge. I could be the best cop there ever was, but if the system we were operating in was malfunctioning, then it would be limited. The impact had to go deeper, not just surface level. If there was another police officer who was the best there ever was, serving during the time our home was burglarized, would they have prevented the crime? Probably not. And it's not just on them. It was on a structure that led to criminal street gangs and impoverished families. That officer might have responded well, perhaps even found out who did it. But it would keep happening as long as young men felt their best option was to join a gang and harm others.

Sometimes, if you want to change the world, you can't just keep playing the same games everyone is playing. Even if you are the best at playing that game. It's still the same game. You have to change the game sometimes, flip it upside down, drop it on the ground, pick it up, and redesign it into something better.

> **Sometimes, if you want to change the world, you can't just keep playing the same games everyone is playing.**

That was my new plan heading into my sophomore year. It was helping me secure my objective of impacting as many people as possible.

At the same time I was rethinking my entire career, I was also rethinking where I would live after my first year in the dorms.

College Livin'

Freshmen at Chico State were required to do one year in the dorms, but after that, they're forced out into local residential housing. A few of us guys from the same floor in the Shasta dorms came together to get a four-bedroom apartment a mile from campus. The guys weren't big partiers, so I thought it was perfect for staying locked in. But they also knew how to have a good time and turn up when you just needed to express yourself. It was a good balance, homeostasis. Living with them was the funniest year of my life. I have never laughed that much.

My roommate Seabass was from the Bay Area, out of Stockton, but also Lodi. We'd make fun of him for always switching up on us about where he's from. "Wait, are you from Stockton or Lodi? Pick one," we'd jokingly say. Seabass had a unique comedic sense of dark humor that was also creative. He was the best at saying something that wasn't funny and then spinning it off by trying to break down the science behind why it was funny, which didn't make it any funnier, but his playful, conscious effort was a funny act. "It's funny because if you combine this element with that one, and on top of this one, it makes sense. You get it, right? It's funny, right?" as he tries to shake your hand in a joking gesture of validation. My other roommate Berto came from the neighborhoods out of San Diego. He knew the slang and the down-the-block comedy of Hot Cheeto fingers and toxic masculinity. Berto and I related to each other the most. We also had a roommate from Napa, Tim, who had a country, goofy vibe to him. He was notorious for making peanut butter and honey burritos with flour tortillas straight out of the fridge.

It was such a great group, man.

One of the memories that I can write about was when Berto asked me the existential question, "What gets you up in the morning?" It was a question from one of his classes that debated the meaning of life. He wanted to see what inspires me, drives me to start my day. Something bigger than myself. He knew I was hardworking, so there had to be a purpose to my routine that ran deep.

So I meaningfully responded, "A banana."

Berto started busting up while we were perusing the Safeway grocery store. I looked at him with a serious, surprised face because I meant it. Every morning those days, I would wake up, jump off my bunk bed, slowly walk to the kitchen as I stumbled from the early morning vertigo, and grab a banana to start my day. I'd still be half asleep while eating it. It was like my morning coffee. Seabass would reenact the way my morning routine looked, making us all laugh.

From the movie nights to the cheat days to the turn-ups, to the imaginary skits and impersonations, to the inside jokes and brotherly love, to the debates about washing dishes, it was all a movie. Living in an apartment with close friends you get along with was a true gift. When you live with family, by yourself, or with a partner, you have to plan your hangouts with friends. When you live with friends, informal hangouts happen every day, all the time.

Coming back from class or work was always a vibe. You'd walk into our place, take a spot on our second-hand black leather couch, and just start clowning on something that happened. It was a comedic paradise.

Little did I know, I was going to need all those laughs to cope with the painful news about my father's health.

Dad's Diagnosis

The summer before my sophomore year, my dad had a routine colonoscopy. Dad took health seriously. He worked out every morning, ate real clean: lean meats, vegetables, olive oil, potatoes, brown rice, and went to sleep on time every night. He was intentional about his body and loved watching the Dr. Oz show. But after the colonoscopy, the doctor came in and delivered the painful news: stage four colon cancer. There ain't no more stages after stage four, my guy. *That's the final one.* The survival rates for stage four colon cancer are approximately 13%.[20] Stage 4 is like, *shit, I might have to get my things in order.*

My dad couldn't believe it. A terminal illness diagnosis, despite all the effort he put into his health. The doctor gave him six months to live—just like that. The strongest guy I knew, my male role model, suddenly looked mortal now.

Dad was always my protector. One of my fondest memories of my Dad protecting me was when we went dirt biking with a few of his buddies. It was out in the desert. I was about 10. The terrain was rough, rocky hills on dusty plains. My Dad and I shared a tri-wheeler dirt bike. It was a hefty machine, weighing around 300 pounds of metal. We took it up a steep hill. I was sitting in front while my Dad was behind me, steering. The incline was so sharp that midway the bike just lost power. You could hear the engine go silent as it made one last puff of effort—*poof*. Due to the steep angle, we fell back in silence onto the rocky ground. And the bike was falling back as well, headed straight for us. I was in front of my Dad, so I would be the first one hit. I remember watching the bike in slow motion, making its way through the air with a crash course straight to my head. I didn't even raise my hands. I was like, "Uh oh, I'm about to get wrecked." Then, in the final moments, these arms come from around me, stretched out fingers, veins popping from the forearms. My Dad's hands caught the bike in its tracks and then tossed it to the side. The dirt bike tumbled in the dust, saving me from a serious accident.

He was my protector then. He pulled out superhuman strength to help his son. But now, the tables were turned. He was the one who needed saving.

After the cancer diagnosis, I told him, "Dad, you gotta fight this somehow, someway. I need you at my graduation." I was 19 then, barely figuring out what it meant to be a man. Now, I had to be over eight hours away from him while he fought for his life.

Bruh, I didn't think making it out the neighborhood would be this hard. First, an identity crisis. Second, basketball was taken from me. Third, my health went to shit. And fourth, my dad was dying. Boom, boom, boom, boom. Four life disruptors, tearing through me like butter. *Almost like a neighborhood omen coming after me for leaving it behind.*

I was ready to come home. Come home to the neighborhood. Ask for forgiveness and mercy. Support my dad. Figure out my health. Rekindle my love for the game.

Good news finally came my way: My transfer paperwork came through. I was accepted into multiple CSUs. The 'coming home' campaign was about to take off. I committed to Long Beach State, which was the second acceptance letter I got from them. I wasn't going to reject them this time. I had just one more semester left in my sophomore year before I could initiate the transfer. My dad was hyped too, already telling his friends I was coming back. He was ready to have his boy back in town—his only son, his prodigy.

But the transfer didn't make it in time.

In February 2017, my dad passed away in a slow, painful death, where he was just skin and bones. He spent his final two weeks in hospice, counting his days down. I was by his side every day during the final moments. It was so hard to see him that weak. He was always my mirror of strength and invincibility.

After he passed, I took two weeks off school, mourning his loss in my childhood room. My sister Lisa slept in my room every night on the ground to check in on me periodically and prevent me from being alone. It wasn't just my pain anymore. It was hers too. She has always been there for me in my darkest moments.

I went surfing at Huntington Beach during that time. It was a foggy morning, with rain coming down. The waves were rocky. The beach was empty. I took out the shortboard my dad gave me and paddled out. Once I made it past the crash zone, I just laid on my board. I hardly took any waves; more there to feel the ocean and its energy. It was just like a scene from the movie *Dear John*, where the son goes surfing in the rain after his pops dies. My dad taught me how to surf, and this was the same beach where we first went riding. As I rested on the board, waves tossing me up and down, I weighed my options. I wondered what would happen if I let myself float away and drown in the sea. I imagined the scenarios, while quietly sinking away. No one was out there. It would take a while for someone to find out. It would be easy.

Shoulders rested on the board. Chin tucked down. Eyes staring out. The occasional waves and raindrops blurred my vision. I started seeing life as a spectator. What would the world look like without me? My mind traveled to different scenes following my death. I saw my mom completely broken by the loss of her baby boy. Her life would never be the same. Everything she did to raise me would go to waste.

I couldn't let her efforts go down the drain. I snapped back to the surface and paddled to shore.

As I was getting ready to head back to college, one of my cousins called to see how I was holding up. "The school will let you take off an entire semester for bereavement. You don't have to go back. That shit is serious, take whatever you need." I thought about it. But I knew my dad wouldn't have wanted that. He would've wanted me to finish up. He was even hesitant when I left school to be with him in hospice. And if I had missed a semester, my transfer would have been revoked.

So I went back to work. Clocked in late, missing the first couple of weeks of the semester. It was going to be hard to catch up. But I embraced the struggle. That last semester of my sophomore year was for Dad. I chased perfection, making straight A's my objective, no matter how much I needed to catch up. I've never worked harder in school. And I got it, nothing but A's, in honor of Pops.

I got you, Dad.

And then, it was time to head home. Back to the neighborhood I came from. Even if it was too late for my dad.

Made it Out?

Making it out of the neighborhood wasn't how I had pictured it. It wasn't this esoteric, transcendence into a whole new level of life. Now, you could argue I was just dealt some tough cards. Someone else might have left the neighborhood, played their dream sport, lived out their glory years, met a lifelong partner, and built a pathway to financial freedom. That could very well happen.

But I want to make this clear: Leaving the neighborhood isn't a divine solution that will bring you the heavyweight championship belt of life. You might fight for that belt better in the ring you know than the one you don't—home-court advantage. The elusive dream of leaving an area guarantees riches and glory, rests on the idea that the entire problem is external. It's more complex than that. You can influence your environment instead of letting it shape you. Shape it yourself. *The journey starts inside you.*

Yes, go explore. Live in new places, travel, and seek new adventures. I'm not saying don't do that. What I am saying is—don't let your external environment *control* you. Don't let it alienate you. Don't let it take away your power. Hold on to your power, regardless of whether it means staying in the neighborhood or going somewhere brand new. It's not about either-or. That feeling of belonging was always inside you. Running away from problems isn't a sure way to solve them. You have to confront them. *You have to face the flames.*

You are the creator of your surroundings. If they aren't up to par, do whatever you can to make them better. Don't succumb to them. Yeah, escape poverty, violence, and the stressors of your neighborhood. But do you have to leave to do that? Maybe. Depends on your situation. Ask yourself: How can I best solve these problems? Do I need to be immersed in them to understand the ins and outs? Or do I need to step away and find a safer enclave to have peace of mind before giving back to the community that I know and love?

That's why it's not *just* about making it out. It's also about making it better. They are intertwined. Integrated. Interrelated. They don't have to be separate. They aren't binary. It isn't mutually exclusive. It isn't one or the other.

I thought I made it out by going to college up North. That meant success to me at the time. Everyone back home respected me for having an opportunity to leave. Going off to college is a beautiful thing. Especially when it's centered around gaining an education to benefit your neighborhood. But I was leaving just to get the fuck out. I wasn't leaving to acquire skills that I could use for my community's advantage. I was running away, not on a mission or expedition.

The musical-inspired movie *In the Heights* paints this picture perfectly. Nina, a young girl from the *vecindario* of Washington Heights, goes off to the prestigious Stanford University—far from home. Everyone in the neighborhood crowned her as the one who was able to make it out. But after her first year, she dropped out. Nina felt out of place in that elite environment. She was mistaken for a waitress rather than a high-caliber student, and her father was spending every penny he had on tuition. It's only after coming home and reconnecting with her neighborhood that she finds a new sense of purpose as to why she was out there. "Maybe Stanford isn't a way out. It's a way back," Nina said. She realized her time at Stanford was to get an education that she could put to good use in service to Washington Heights, not to leave it behind. The neighborhood handed her a why. *There was purpose to the sacrifice*. Going off to college wasn't an escape. It was a mission.

There was purpose to the sacrifice.

The main character, Usnavi, came to the same realization. "We work so hard trying to get there that we forget about what's right here," he says. Usnavi tirelessly worked to escape Washington Heights and go back to the island where his dad had raised him. Thanks to the help of his friends and his lover, Usnavi's dream was brought to life in the neighborhood around him. It wasn't on an island in some faraway land.

Usnavi's lover, Vanessa, had a similar conquest of making it out of Washington Heights. She got an expensive apartment in Manhattan, in the vicinity of the high-end fashion industry. After moving, she noticed her creative spirit had disappeared. The ingenious juices she once had for clothing, garments, and color all washed away once she escaped to a sterile enclosure. After going on a walk in Washington Heights, searching for answers, Vanessa's creativity starts roaring back. The inspiration stemmed from the culture of art in *her neighborhood.*

Home created and rekindled her talent for artistry.

My inspiration to change the neighborhood came from making it back.

(In my dorm room with college basketball dreams on my mind— Go Pro photo from my roommate Steph)

(Chico State Shasta 3 Dorms—May 2016)

(Dad and I at a Laker game only a few months before he died)

MADE IT BACK

I found myself in the concrete jungle of dangerous intersections and tagged-up alleys once again. I moved back in with my mom at the PCLs. Everyone knew I hadn't accomplished my dream of playing college basketball, and they knew my dad had just died. And my face was still looking like Kino der Toten for acne crawlers. It was a humbling fall from the last year of high school when I was on top of the world. Now, I was back in my same old room—battle-scarred emotionally, physically, mentally, socially, and spiritually. I had no choice but to *get back to work*.

My first duty was honing in on my career change. I had to rebuild my skills since all my experience was geared toward becoming a cop. But I decided I didn't want to simply follow the policies of the criminal justice system as another soldier on the battlefield. I wanted to be the one crafting the rules—the battle lines, the war zones, and the decisions that led to war in the first place. I wanted to be a lawyer.

I mentioned this idea to my dad a few months before he passed. I was on the phone with him, walking around campus, right in front of the university police department where I worked. He was the first person I called to talk about this potential shift.

"Dad, I think I don't want to be a police officer anymore. I think I want to be a lawyer so I can change the policies of the system," I said, hesitating, almost as if I was asking a question.

I heard some background noise as if he had stopped to sit down. Then he responded in a supportive tone, "Is that right?" Those rhetorical questions were more for him to let it settle a bit.

"Well, it sounds good to me. You got this."

I loved talking to him because he really listened. To this day, I've never met a better listener. He was genuinely curious. At holiday gatherings, he'd talk with my cousins and ask what they were up to. Dad always got into the details, asking them questions about their job or school that most would never care about. He loved giving people the space to just ramble about something they were passionate about.

Those life decisions always went through him first. Sometimes, you need people to simply listen, not force advice on you. Dad would allow me to talk through something, figuring out I already had the answer in mind. I didn't realize how much I leaned on his supportive ear until he was gone.

Thinking LSAT

I started studying for the Law School Admission Test (LSAT) almost every day. That test made me realize how limited my reading, writing, comprehension, and reasoning skills were. I started off scoring pretty low, with a 141 on my first practice test.

I ran into a girl at a Starbucks and noticed she had some LSAT tests in her hand. I interjected and asked how the studying was going. She put me on to these two guys named Nathan and Ben, who created the prep courses Fox LSAT and Strategy Prep, respectively. They also co-hosted a podcast called *Thinking LSAT*. Those courses and podcasts helped me catch up with people who loved reading as kids and grew up in neighborhoods with strong literacy skills.

When I wasn't in the classroom, I was grinding for the LSAT, putting in at least two hours a day, pounding away. In total, I logged over 1,000 hours to become a beast at that test. It changed how I read, wrote, thought, and reasoned. At my peak, I scored 168 on my practice test, which placed me in the top 10% of test takers and good enough for the most prestigious law schools.

Staying consistent at studying took real motivation. Dr. Eric Thomas, the Hip-Hop preacher, had these motivational YouTube videos that I watched daily. My go-to one was *Westbrook Theory*. It broke down Russell Westbrook's legendary season after Kevin Durant betrayed him.

In 2016, Durant left Westbrook and the Oklahoma City Thunder to join Steph Curry and the Golden State Warriors. Prior to his departure, the Thunder were just one win away from beating the Warriors in the playoffs, and yet Durant gave up and joined his competitor for the following season. The Warriors already had the best regular-season record in NBA history, and now they were adding one of the best players on the planet. Durant betrayed Westbrook. Reportedly, he only texted Westbrook to say he was headed out to Golden State.

The move lit an inferno inside Westbrook.

He went on to have the most dominant regular-season performance I have ever seen: averaging a triple-double with 30+ points, 10+ assists, and 11+ rebounds. He won MVP that year and shattered a plethora of NBA records.

Instead of dwelling in sorrow and pain after a brother turned his back on him, Russell turned it up a notch. He pulled out the greatest performance of his life, electrifying the world. Russell did what everyone said was impossible. Fans and players were in absolute awe of the greatness he was pulling out, night after night. Russell moved on from the heartache and capitalized on the moment.

Dr. Eric Thomas used the Westbrook saga to encourage others to *forget those things that are behind you and move toward your greatness*. A bolt of energy shot through my stomach every time I watched that video. I saw my own struggles in it. It's something I still watch to this day.

I was letting go of the traumas from my first years of college and moving toward my dream of Harvard Law School. It was my dream school and the hardest one to get into.

My mom was so proud of her *mijo's* new path. Immigrant parents often dream of their first-generation kids becoming doctors and lawyers. Some of my mom's family even started calling me *licenciado* out of respect for my future law career.

See You In the Neighborhood

When I was a junior at Long Beach State, sitting in a political science class—black beanie on, Pro Club and chain, back in my element—a guest speaker came through to talk about a local grassroots campaign. See, this is why guest speakers are so important.

His name was Jared Milrad, and he was running for Long Beach City Council District 7, which represents the Westside of Long Beach, an area I knew like the back of my hand. The presentation, solid. The speech, solid. The mission, *phenomenal*. He was pushing for cleaner air on the Westside and a change in guard to cultivate new energy at the table. He wanted to make those neighborhoods better than they've ever been.

I remember how he talked about growing up on the East Coast of the U.S. and comparing it to the work he wanted to do on the West Coast. I asked him, "Which is better, West Coast or East Coast?" He hesitated at first, explaining his upbringing playing a part, but ultimately responding, "I think West Coast." It was the right answer. He gestured to me, "Good question." I sharply responded, "Good answer." The class started laughing, and he had no idea that the snobby student with the beanie and chains was going to help the campaign out.

At the time, I wasn't doing much besides going to class and studying for the LSAT. I needed to get involved with something because graduation was knocking at the door.

I decided to join their Civic Fellowship program to help bring peace to the Westside. During the campaign trail, I immediately went knocking on doors right outside my old stomping grounds. I was running into people from elementary school, middle school, and high school all in one day, talking to them about a new campaign trying to change the game for the neighborhood. I was good at it. I was organizing my community, locking in votes for this young candidate who wasn't from Long Beach but had a fire in him that I respected.

It was a runoff election, head-to-head with an incumbent (someone already holding the position). The opponent had every advantage. We were the underdogs, *just how I liked it*. They were the status quo, *exactly where I wanted them*.

We knocked on every door in the area, maybe three or four times. People were tired of seeing us.

One storyline we focused on was the fact that Westside children's asthma rates were twice the national average, and the average life expectancy for residents was significantly lower than that of East Long Beach.[21]

Jared spoke to one homeowner who lived along the 710 freeway. A piece of tire from the diesel trucks had flown into their yard, hot to the touch. They were demanding greater environmental accountability, and Jared was there to help make sure that happened. Funny enough, one of their daughters was someone I'd gone to elementary school with. It was Camila. The same girl who made fun of me for wearing the same shorts every day. Crazy full circle.

Despite our focus on clean air and an effort to change City Hall, some people hated us. One time, we knocked on a door where a tall, bald White dude—swastika tattooed on his head—answered it. He saw the flyers in our hands and immediately yelled at us, "I hate that guy!"

Jared, in an awkward, calm tone, replied, "That guy is me." Then the dude slammed the door in our faces. If there was anyone we wanted to get hate from, it was going to be from someone like him.

Others thought Jared was too young for the role, despite being in his mid-30s. Some said they couldn't vote for him because their religious beliefs conflicted with Jared's sexual orientation. Jared was married to a man, and he was a proud advocate for the LGBTQ community.

But plenty of families were excited for a change in guard. We hosted meet-and-greets wherever people would have us. Jared and the campaign manager, Serafin, worked their asses off, but we came up short in the end. He received 4,166 votes against the opponent's 4,733. Close, but no cigar.

Still, I won the experience of learning what it's like to support your local neighborhoods. The campaign was built on the idea of becoming a change agent for the Westside. I loved it. One of the best lines from Jared's campaign video was, "See you in the neighborhood," right before he walked off, headed down a block of homes nestled into a community. Jared helped me believe that you can make the world the way it should be, and you can do it locally, too. It made me start thinking about serving the neighborhood I came from. That marinated in my mind while I was getting ready to leave for a study abroad class.

Taxi Sono Qui!

At the end of my junior year of college, I signed up for a study abroad program.

I wanted to study abroad because my sister Lisa had done it in Vietnam. Just like going to the same high school as her, I tried to copy her once again. It felt like a mandatory part of college, something every student should experience. Plus, the program was based in Italy. Growing up, I watched all the *Jersey Shore* episodes where they roamed the cobblestone streets of Florence. I wanted to recreate those scenes. If I had to emulate anyone, it was for sure Pauly D, something I would remind the other classmates to make sure they didn't steal my character.

Studying abroad isn't something neighborhood kids usually get to do because of how expensive it was. The financial aid grants didn't cover it, so I took out a couple of subsidized loans to pay for the trip. I knew my older, wiser self would be ok paying off the debts of my younger, reckless, wandering self. I ran the numbers, and the math added up.

The trip cost me about $7,000, and not everyone agreed with my decision. My friend Ever, while we were hanging out in our college society office, kept it real with me.

"You're taking out loans to study abroad?" He shook his head. "Don't be stupid man...You'll be in debt."

He was just looking out for me, coming from a risk-averse place. I stubbornly responded, "I know. But I have to go explore the world in this phase of my life. This is it. I won't get another opportunity to study abroad as an undergrad. My older self will pay it back and thank me for it."

Pride has committed mistakes in my life, but this wasn't one of them.

Ever was from the neighborhood. Growing up in poverty on the lower Westside of Long Beach, he couldn't fathom why I would pay for something that seemed like a luxury.

I knew studying abroad wasn't something that would be offered in any other phase of my life. *I had to do it right then and there.*

Some of those decisions you make in your early 20s impact your life for decades to come. You make them with the best evidence you have at the time, but you don't really know if it's the right path until years later.

Bill Perkins, author of *Die with Zero*, shares a decision he regretted in his early 20s. Bill had just entered the workforce and was trying to make a name for himself. He was in hustle mode, sharing a small place with a friend in New York, saving every penny he had. His roommate, Jason, spontaneously decided to go backpacking through Europe to explore the world. And Jason was going to borrow money to make it happen, *just like I did*. Bill rejected Jason's offer to join him, citing the need to move up the ladder at his job and not risk the loan payments.

Over twenty years later, it serves as a life lesson for Bill. Jason traveled around Europe, gathering wisdom that can't be bought, meeting people he'd remember forever, and forging stories worth sharing around the campfire. After Jason came back, he had the same job alongside Bill and fell slightly behind in their company, but not much. Meanwhile, Jason returned much "richer in stories, romances, experiences, and lifelong friends." Bill wished he had gone with him during that era of his life.

When the opportunity finally came back around for Bill to go backpacking in Europe, he wasn't in the same phase of his life anymore for that youth hostel living and taking long gaps. It wasn't the same experience, he noted. The era had passed him by. It wasn't as rich of an experience as his friend Jason had, who did it at a precious moment.

Bill talks about the phases of opportunities to do things like go backpacking with your roommate in your development years, which don't reap the same benefits later. You have to seize the moment and set up a system where you don't leave things on the table, both in terms of experiences and finances, hence the title, *Die with Zero*.

As I reflect on the moment when I decided to go into debt to study abroad, I'm glad my younger self took the risk. Yes, I still have a few small loans being paid off, but nothing crazy. I knew when to work my ass off in school and when to go explore the world at a high level. *Giving and getting everything life had to offer.* The memories of that trip were priceless. Now, I am not saying you should just go spend all your money on memories. Financial literacy is a struggle in the neighborhood. I remember homies foolishly spending thousands of dollars just to impress others. There's a time and place where those dollars are well saved on building your future and then well spent on enriching life memories that elevate who you are. This study abroad trip was the latter.

We traveled to Rome, Florence, Perugia, and Assisi, where we studied forensic science. We investigated the Amanda Knox case and the Monster of Florence, speaking to detectives and police officers to get to the bottom of the case. I spent mornings half-awake, hungover from the prior night's adventures, which included going to the clubs the Jersey Shore cast went to. The walks to class featured statues of the greats: Da Vinci, Michelangelo, and Brunelleschi, all in the birthplace of the Italian Renaissance.

Not only did that program help me step out of my enclave of American communities, but it also gave me a lifelong friend: My boy, Ed. The same name as my dad, as if the universe were handing me a new family member for my life's journey. Ed and I were a travel dyad, always making fun of someone or something. We were roommates the entire trip and had each other's backs during wild nights out on the town.

I also fell for a girl in the study abroad class, completely obsessed. My first real feelings for someone since my high school sweetheart. I didn't know it was love at the time, but I figured it out a long time later. It was a different type of romance. We shared affection on the grounds of the Roman Empire, kissed in front of the Eiffel Tower, and shared sangria adventures in Spain.

The trip and the romance only lasted that summer, but it changed me. It helped me see beyond my little half-square-mile neighborhood. The world was so vast, with so much to see, share, and do.

As my grandma would always tell me, "You got the travel bug, young man."

SHPE Happens

My senior year of college was when I came into my own—when I discovered who I was and what I believed in. Senior year is like a lifelong friend: You can be yourself around them because you've been through it all together. You've seen each other at your worst, so you don't hold back that authentic self.

My new lifelong friends came from a corny lil college society full of strangers who were trying to become engineers. Basketball served as my bridge once again. I joined the Society of Hispanic Professional Engineers (SHPE) because my high school friend Ever said I could play intramural basketball with them. That society became more than just basketball teammates; it gifted me with some of the best memories of my glory years and lifelong friendships.

I was the only one in the society who wasn't an engineer, just there to play on the same basketball team. Fresh off leaving Chico State, I needed new friends, especially since I wasn't going out much because of my grind bag. All the friends I made in my first two years of college were now eight hours away. It was time to draft a new squad. And for my first pick in the SHPE draft, I became homies with whoever hung out in the club's office.

I would nervously enter when Ever wasn't with me and take a seat on a crumpled-up leather couch. A few people playing video games on their laptops, and someone else warming up their food in the microwave. I felt a bit out of place at first because I wasn't an engineer, and it wasn't my club. Fortunately, they accepted me with open arms. I knew we became close when we started making fun of each other. That was our measurement indicator for close friends.

We had our own office on campus, where we would hang out in between classes, complain about professors, throw down a few cold ones, watch the Laker game, study for an exam, and just clown on each other. You need those places to serve as your social anchor. From busting open bottles before our 8 am class to arguing about who's the best player in the NBA, SHPE gave me the social enclave I needed at the time.

ACLU Internship

During my run for lawyer, I dreamed of working for the largest public interest law firm in the nation: the American Civil Liberties Union (ACLU). I'd read about them and had seen them mentioned on TV. People either hated or loved them, but everybody knew them, and I wanted to do big-time work on a big-time stage.

I told people about my dream to speak it into existence, and someone once said, "Oh yeah, interning for the ACLU was my dream too, but it never happened. It's just too hard to get." They wished me luck anyway.

Of course, a lot of people wanted to work there. *Why would they pick this neighborhood kid?*

I put in several applications online, hoping to get selected for one of their internship programs. I never heard back. With my last semester of college approaching, I needed an internship to finish up my degree, and I wanted it to be at the ACLU's downtown Los Angeles office. So I decided to pull up in person.

On a hot day, I drove to downtown LA in my only suit from Macy's. I walked up to their front desk, sweat dripping off my nose. The front desk attendant refused my request to speak to one of the attorneys. He told me to come back. Little did he know how long my drive was.

I came back a few weeks later with the same awkward suit, same awkward request. This time, the attendant handed me a card with someone's email. It was a lawyer on the Education Equity team. I emailed him, sent my resume, and asked to volunteer. He replied, "Unfortunately, we get many more volunteer inquiries than we can accept." And I never heard from him again. I lost some hope, feeling like another failed dream.

But that wasn't the end of my ACLU story.

A few weeks after losing hope in landing that internship, I was doing homework in my room when my momma walked in and asked me if I wanted to attend a community event with her. It was a political club meeting at an IHOP across town. I had never been to these meetings before, so it was interesting that she invited me. An easy no was about to murmur out of my mouth, but I hesitated. I looked back at my desk full of case reviews and LSAT tests and thought, *Aw, what the hell. Might as well get a break from grinding.*

We were at the back of the IHOP in a secluded section for events—silver spoons clattering against ceramic plates. You could see people munching on the first bite of their hamburgers and cutting into a stack of pancakes as we waited. The organizers approached the center of the open tables and announced that they had a civil rights attorney giving a special presentation.

You wouldn't believe it. The presenter was Dr. Amir Whitaker from the ACLU Education Equity Office. His talk was on school suspensions and expulsions. It all lined up, and the topic was something that hit close to home.

I was suspended in the fifth grade at Jackie Robinson Academy. A kid pushed me to the ground on the basketball court, so I had to rack him up with a few haymakers. I was in a good number of fights back then. Anywhere from putting a dude in a headlock and punching him in the forehead to fighting a tall homie, where I would jump in the air as I delivered the Superman punch.

The turmoil at home between my parents' battles and financial struggles made me lash out at school. That's why it's so important to look at the totality of a student's life before rendering judgment.

They suspended me for a day and sent me home to do nothing—just chill, I guess. The other kid wasn't suspended, even though he got some good ones in on me when he was kicking me from the ground. I spent that day at home alone, watching *King of Queens* and *Seinfeld* on the couch. I had missed serious class time, so when I got back the next day, I was eager to make up for it. I asked my teacher what work I missed. She always started the day with a nasty attitude, as if she hated her job. She looked at me and, I kid you not, said, "No, you can't make up the work. You missed your chance, and it is your fault that you missed class." I did my time, served the suspension at home, and returned ready to make amends. But instead of helping me get back on track, I was pushed out even further.

It sucked back then. But ten years later, that story helped me out at this random IHOP.

I listened closely to Dr. Whitaker break down how the Long Beach Unified School District (LBUSD) was pushing students out through suspensions and expulsions. I asked a big-time question, showing I was tuned in. I prepared my elevator pitch in my head. When the event wrapped up, I hung back while others spoke to him.

My turn was up. He was tall, about 6'2", with an Afro shaved up on the sides and dyed purple at the tips. The look in his eyes conveyed both humility and wisdom simultaneously. He was fairly young, in his 30s, but his wisdom revealed he had lived many lives.

I gave him the pitch I had in the tank. "That was a great presentation. I was also pushed out of the classroom for disciplinary reasons, including an off-campus suspension for fighting. This hits home for me. It's personal."

He nodded as if he could relate to the sentiment. "Wow, man. Thanks for sharing. Yeah, LBUSD has real issues with expulsions and suspensions. We have to hold them accountable and use stories like yours as tools to change their discipline standards."

It was a lob, and I threw it down. "And that's exactly what I've been trying to do. I've shown up at your office multiple times to try to volunteer, but no one has ever gotten back to me. I would love to support your work by interning and being a part of the solution."

His head tilted back slightly in surprise. "That's great to hear. We could use all the intern support we can get. I'll give you my card. Send me your resume. Then we'll go from there."

I sent it over. A few weeks later, I got an invitation to meet the team. The lawyer I'd been emailing back when I initially showed up at the ACLU, hoping for a shot, was a part of that same team Dr. Whitaker was on. Now, I was reintroducing myself. I wasn't embarrassed by the rejections. I was proud of them. Proud that I kept showing up out of the blue, only to be rejected time and time again. I was a weed that kept growing out of the concrete walls of that office. They sprayed me away at the front door, but I found some life in the crevice of the inside. After I met everyone on the team, they officially started the process to bring me on board. Boom. Just like that. A big-time W. One I wanted.

I was slowly building my path of making it out of my neighborhood as a big-time lawyer.

I started putting in work at that law firm. Showing up fired up. I loved being in those meetings with several high-profile attorneys, where we brainstormed lawsuits to make the education system better. I researched how much schools spent on law enforcement in comparison to art education, the number of students arrested for school disciplinary issues, and anything else related to education equity and the school-to-prison pipeline. I worked alongside a bright intern who was attending UCLA, Avery, and was one of the best readers and writers I had ever met. She was *zoom zoom* when reviewing memos and briefs, so good that they had her edit the next big ACLU report.

I was still struggling to transcend years of hating to read because "it wasn't cool." Being around Avery no doubt inspired me to go harder and make up for younger me.

Dr. Whitaker and the team uncovered some crazy numbers: 1.7 million students in the U.S. attended a school with a cop but no counselor; three million had a cop but no nurses; and 10 million had a cop but no social worker.[22] These numbers went viral. It showed me how data can tell a story. Helping put that report out (albeit with very little help from me) was something I'd be proud of for years to come.

1.7 million
students are in schools with cops, but no counselors.

3 million
students are in schools with cops, but no nurses.

6 million
students are in schools with cops, but no school psychologists.

10 million
students are in schools with cops, but no social workers.

Source: U.S. Department of Education, Civil Rights Data Collection, 2015-16

(Dr. Whitaker's data snapshot that he put out during my time on his team)

Seven Continents

I wasn't just in awe of the work Dr. Whitaker was doing at the ACLU. I was in awe of his personal accomplishments. He was a lawyer, had a PhD, founded a nonprofit (Project Knucklehead), wrote a book (*Escaping the Trap*), and traveled to 30 countries before turning 30. He was checking off every box in his go-around of life. Usually, there are tradeoffs: You are either underlived or underskilled, as Chris Williamson noted in his *Modern Wisdom* podcast. But Amir was both well-lived and well-skilled. Everything he was doing inspired me, and I wanted to travel the world just like him.

One day in the office, I told him, "I'm going to travel to 30 countries before I turn 30, just like you." He lifted his head in a show of approval, "Cool. Yeah, it's so worth it."

I was fresh off my Europe trip with a handful of countries in my back pocket as a 21-year-old. I could make it. However, the goal didn't really feel like mine, and I thought that visiting 30 countries would make the trips more transactional. So I changed my mind and decided to focus on continents.

I remember as a kid in 3rd grade reciting the seven continents of the world. To really travel the entire world, you have to go to every continent. I knew traveling helped me download wisdom from other people, places, and customs. So I thought, *What if I downloaded the wisdom of what it's like living all around the world, on every continent?* If I could travel to every single continent before turning 30, I'd know what this planet really has to offer. So I made it my goal for the decade.

The Walk

Interns were never given parking at the ACLU, so I had to find spots on the streets of Downtown Los Angeles. I enjoyed those walks to my car. Some of your best ideas come to you during a walk. Albert Einstein was known for his daily walks around the Princeton campus, where his thought experiments contributed to theoretical physics. Steve Jobs was known for his walks around Apple, where frustration with technology would often give rise to innovative gadgets that we use today. Long walks, late nights, and time in nature unleash my most creative and introspective moments.

On a chilly late night, as I walked about 30 minutes to my car through the juxtaposition of high-rises and homeless encampments, I began to think about where I was investing my time and energy.

I was putting my talents and skills to use at this national law firm. It was meaningful work for the larger landscape, but it didn't have any direct effect on the Washington Neighborhood. The neighborhood that raised me. I was driving away from my neighborhood to be in downtown

L.A., putting on for a prestigious law firm. *I had forgotten that I was back.* Back living in my community. Yet, I wasn't putting in any work for it. It hit me. Another epiphany moment. Right there, mid-walk, mid-thought.

My next venture had to focus on the neighborhood I grew up in.

On that walk, I started brainstorming what I could do back home. How could I do it? What does my community need most, and what can I best provide?

I started talking to myself about the things I was best at: "I'm good at basketball, have been playing all my life, averaging 20 points a game in this intramural league. I'm also really good at education, about to earn a bachelor's degree with Magna Cum Laude, something uncommon in my neighborhood."

I had to find a way to merge the two strengths, basketball and education, into a weapon for impact. That's when the idea came to me: *Basketball is my bucket strength, and education is my book strength.* In college, all I did was read books and play basketball. And what changed my life? That youth program that I had to take a long-ass bus ride for. What if I didn't need that bus ride? What if my homies could have joined? What if it were free? What if my neighborhood had those same high-caliber programs? I could utilize my talents of buckets (basketball) and books (education) and form my own youth program in an area people were scared to do programming in: Books & Buckets in the Washington Neighborhood.

On that late-night walk to my car, that game-changing idea was given life. A seed ready to be planted.

This idea threw a curveball at my career. I went from police officer to lawyer, and then landed as an aspiring neighborhood change-maker. College years are full of back-and-forths, never-minds, and maybe-nots. *It's OK to bounce around before snuggling in.* It's actually better to jump around instead of holding tight in a place you don't like. You just have to keep trying new things. Everything's an experiment.

For anyone trying to figure things out, I've found the following framework to be helpful:

Three Tries & You're In

Try #1 See if it's needed: try and see if it's something needed in the world. Is there a want for it? Is it growing? Can you see yourself in any current positions? This establishes its utility and demand.

Try #2 See if you love it: try and see if you have a love for it. Is it a passion? Does it run deep? Would you enjoy waking up on a Saturday morning for it? This measures the fire for it.

Try #3 See if you're a natural at it: try and see if you have a knack for it. Does it come naturally to you, or is it an uphill battle? Do your talents align with the day-to-day tasks required? This gauges your alignment with it.

If the career checks all three, then you're in. It's for you. Now, all three are not necessary. Meaning, two of them can still make it work. But all three are sufficient for that sweet spot.

Coming back home for school and work put everything into perspective. It's hard to ignore problems when you walk past them every day. I knew there was a need for it. My love was always for my *barrio*, and I had a genuine talent for connecting with the local community. It was right for me.

Coming back made me rethink everything. Living around the stressors of the Washington Neighborhood added urgency to the cause. This is something more elected officials need to understand.

In the documentary *Street Fight*, filmed by Marshall Curry, Cory Booker's run for mayor of Newark is put on full display. There's a scene that shows where Booker lives—a run-down, low-income complex in one of the toughest parts of his district. It was a public housing project called Brick Towers, and Booker moved in after that community elected him to serve on the City Council. Like a magnet on the fridge, Brick Towers was a constant reminder of how much work needed to be done. As the camera follows Booker around the campaign trail, he comments to a group of men outside a laundromat, "Make every politician live in the worst neighborhood in their city. I guarantee the city would turn around a lot quicker."

Look, I'm not saying you have to expose yourself to every stressor to solve them. But you can't be detached. You can't be disconnected from the place that raised you. You can't forget. Brick Towers kept Cory Booker in the loop. The Washington Neighborhood kept me grounded in the realities of my community.

Being back in the neighborhood reminded me of the daily struggle. I was not only in retreat from the tough run up North, but I was reimagining what useful purpose I could have in the world. The idea of starting a nonprofit originated from being tapped into the landscape of my community. Tapped into the pulse of neighborhood resilience.

It's easy to ignore and neglect a place when it no longer holds a constant space in your heart and mind. My neighborhood reminded me where my focus should be.

Making it back made me realize I should make it better.

(Rome, Italy, during my study abroad trip—photo from my classmate Alyssa)

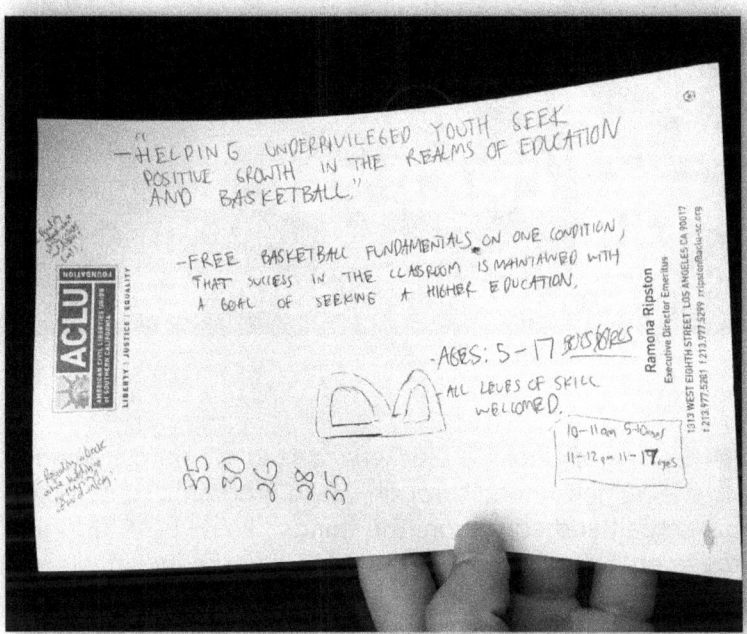

(My intern sketch pads I used to write out the first idea for Books & Buckets)

MADE IT BETTER

The idea of Books & Buckets started off simple: change the neighborhood through youth programs centered on basketball and education, the things I knew best. Bringing these programs to our community would reduce gang violence and build the safe neighborhood I'd always dreamed of. With that dream in mind, I clocked in and got to work. Relentlessly.

Founding (Section 1)

I wanted Books & Buckets to become a nonprofit, funded by donations and grants, so families in our programs would never have to pull out their wallets. But I didn't know much about starting a nonprofit back then. I was a dumb college kid.

After my internship with the ACLU, I graduated from Long Beach State with a Bachelor of Science in Criminology and Criminal Justice. I was named the Jack R. Coler Award recipient, Male Student of the Year, for the College of Health and Human Services' Criminology program. I also had a 3.96 GPA.

But I had no job offers.

I thought if I got straight A's, everyone would want me on their team. That employers would bow before my feet, eager to bring me in. *I couldn't have been more wrong.* I had only applied to five jobs before graduating, thinking most of them would offer me. None of them did. I remember telling a law school intern at the ACLU about the number of jobs I applied for. She laughed at me and said I needed to apply to at least 20. I stubbornly rejected her advice and later learned she was right. This was one occasion where my resistance led to a mistake.

No job offers. A dream of starting a nonprofit with no real knowledge about nonprofits. The soon-to-be college graduate glow was fading. I didn't have much going for me.

Sometimes you have to take a step back before you take a step up.

Graduation Gift

I knew I had to get out of my bubble and celebrate earning my degree—didn't matter if I lacked a steady income. I had planned this months before graduating.

My study abroad buddy Ed and I backpacked throughout Southeast Asia.

Thailand, Cambodia, Vietnam. Our first time living as *mochileros*, backpackers with nothing but a pack on our back and adventure in mind. We stayed at hostels in big cities and small islands, sometimes paying five bucks a night. We saw the Grand Palace in Thailand, Angkor Wat Temple in Cambodia, and Ha Long Bay in Vietnam. We were out there for over a month, teaming up with fellow backpackers we met along the way from Germany, Australia, England, and North Carolina.

One of the wildest trips was *Castaways*, where about forty young backpackers teamed up in Hanoi to spend a few days on a private island in Ha Long Bay. There was no cell phone service on this small, secluded island. It was just food, drinks, water sports, rock climbing, volleyball, and a bunch of people trying to have a good time. I don't have any videos or photos from the trip because the phone was set aside as we enjoyed the ride.

On our way out of Hanoi and heading to Ho Chi Minh, we took an open-top Jeep trip with a couple of girls we met at Castaways and cruised through the Hai Van Pass, a mountain pass known as the best coastal road in the world.

We were livin' the dream. Some of the best nights of my life were spent backpacking in Southeast Asia.

#ProudtobeLBUSD

As we were leaving Cambodia and heading to the airport, I got an email from Jared. It was about another political campaign sparking up. He connected me with someone running a school board campaign for the district that covers West and Central Long Beach. They were looking for a campaign coordinator. Jared recommended me to the campaign team, and they wanted to set up an interview.

School board members make the big decisions for school districts: high-level appointments, setting policies, and approving budgets. This campaign involved the schools I was familiar with: Webster Elementary, Washington Middle School, Jackie Robinson Academy, and Cabrillo High. These were communities I knew very well: Washington and Westside. It was adding up. I had the opportunity to make a positive impact on my local neighborhood and get paid for it. The mission was great. The pay? Weak. But aye, I needed a job.

I interviewed as soon as I got back from my backpacking trip. I met the candidate, Erik Miller, at Polly's Pies restaurant, a corny joint for a coffee and apple pie, located in a more affluent area of Long Beach. We hit it off real quick, sharing similar backgrounds of poverty, gang violence, and a mission to change things around. I could feel his genuine do-good intention.

There's a saying in politics that two types of people try to run for office: people who want to "be someone" or people who want to "do something." I could feel that Erik wanted to do something.

During the campaign, I knocked on the doors of old classmates, teammates, and teachers again. I gave the campaign my absolute all, especially since it was a payback campaign for me.

One of our opponents was tied to the same political establishment that took down Jared in that City Council race I volunteered for. This was an opportunity to prove myself. To prove I was good at what I did. That I could lead a winning campaign. *A second chance.* It was personal.

Once the campaign season started heating up, I was working Monday through Sunday. Saturdays and Sundays were the hardest. That's when all the volunteers rolled in and the events took place. I was easily pulling 12-hour days on the weekends. After work, I'd rush to get ready to hit the club with my boys, dancing all night, talking to girls, and a few hours later, I'd be right back in the office on Sunday morning bright and early, ready to send out a team to go knock on some doors.

I had a team of over 12 field canvassers, seven civic fellows, and a whole bunch of volunteers, including teachers, nurses, counselors, family, and friends. The civic fellowship was something I started, modeled after the fellowship I served in Jared's campaign. I presented the program in several classes at Long Beach State, just as Jared did when I was a student. I was pretty good at starting things that changed my life and making sure they lived on for the next generation.

I even came up with an idea to mirror our connection to the school district. One afternoon, chopping it up with my boy Ed (who would come by and work out of my office), I kept saying how we needed a brand or slogan to hop onto or create—something that stuck with voters. Similar to Jared's "See you in the neighborhood" line which promoted unity with community. We needed a John Cena "You can't see me" type of mic drop. I wanted to show how our candidate was the best option for overseeing our schools. Something to end every video or post with.

Ed and I tried to come up with something, throwing out different made-up catchphrases. I'd lean back into my chair after every suggestion, shaking my head and saying, "Nah, that's weak."

We were thinking too hard. *We were trying to fix the TV by taking it apart when the real problem was that it wasn't plugged in.* The answer was already out there, right in front of our faces.

I knew the strong point of our campaign was that Erik went to school in the district, and the opponent didn't. The opponent didn't even send their kids there. So we had to lead with that point everywhere we went.

Then it clicked. The school district's slogan was "Proud to be LBUSD," a simple, catchy phrase that showed love for the district. Erik was a proud product of the district who planned to send his daughter there. It was something our competitor couldn't claim. So we could say it but they couldn't, fabulous.

So we ran with it. We made sure *#ProudtobeLBUSD* was said in every video, and every post—a constant reminder that we were for the district while the opponent wasn't. It worked. And it made every marketing piece a little bit better.

I worked hard on that campaign, blue-collar style. One night, I even slept in the office. I had worked so late that it didn't make sense for me to go home just to come back a few hours later. I picked a spot on the floor, grabbed my jacket like a blanket, found a random couch pillow, and knocked out. I was loving the grind.

We ended up winning that election in November 2020 with over 15,000 votes. I celebrated with Erik at his mom's house. All those long nights paid off.

I left the campaign after the primary election to get a real job. I needed to make a decent income with benefits and vacation. I was applying to a few different nonprofits, hoping one would take a chance on your boy. Luckily, a local nonprofit believed in me.

I was offered a $40,000 salary job from The Nonprofit Partnership (TNP). I remember doing pull-ups at 14th Street Park, feeling like I had finally made it. Looking back, it wasn't much. But for a 22-year-old from the neighborhood trying to make it in the professional field, I was grateful.

I started in April 2020, working virtually on a laptop and meeting all my new colleagues on Zoom, which randomly turned into the de facto teleconferencing tool that everyone was using. Much of our work involved community members I already knew through my neighborhood involvement. I worked on Best Start, a systems change initiative focused on children ages zero to five and their families. One of my favorite projects was participatory budgeting, where community members got to *participate* in how money was *budgeted* for their neighborhoods. It was an empowering process to see the community take an idea, draft a plan, pitch it to their neighbors for a vote, and if they won, implement the project. The process was often more empowering than the actual projects that got funded themselves.

Participatory Budgeting (PB)

PB originated in Porto Alegre, Brazil, in 1989 as a way to give ordinary people the power over how to spend public dollars for their neighborhoods. As mentioned in Josher Lerner's book, *Everyone Counts: Could 'Participatory Budgeting' Change Democracy*, PB aims to "put the power of the purse back into the community." Lerner highlights how PB rewires the system rather than swapping out one politician for another.

The first PB process in the U.S. took place in Chicago, led by elected official Jon Moore. At the time, Moore had just scraped by in his reelection, winning just 52 percent of the vote. Looking for something new to win back the trust of his residents, he saw PB as an experiment to serve that purpose. After he initiated the PB process in his representative communities, his next reelection was a piece of cake. He won 72 percent of the vote, with PB being cited as the game-changer for voters.

Fast forward to Long Beach in 2013. A Long Beach State professor named Gary Hytrek brings PB to the city by the sea, launching in the Northside at Houghton Park with then-Councilmember Rex Richardson. All the community engagement they initiated in the idea collection phase of the process turned into an informal needs assessment. Even if a project wasn't funded in the PB process, they were able to find other ways to make it happen. The process has continued to gain traction and insert itself in different fund disbursements throughout Long Beach.

I stayed with that nonprofit for a little over a year. We disbursed over $1.2 million in community projects. Throughout that time, I learned how nonprofits operate. I sat in on nonprofit management trainings, learned from nonprofit executive directors, and brought that knowledge back to my neighborhood.

After a year at TNP, salary talks came up. I was a young bull, confident in his intangible abilities to serve the local community. I wanted to get paid more, but they were limited in how much they could pay me due to my title.

I had to make a choice: settle and accept a low-paying job for another year or take a stand for myself. A stand that said my abilities warranted more. After battling in my mind, running scenarios with friends, and intuition seeking for a major life decision, I made my stand. I resigned. And I was fired up.

I wanted to make a statement and bet on myself.

To do that, I had to go off the deep end.

I had to put my back against the wall with no way out but through.

That pressure would bring out the best in me.

I was 23 years old. It was May 2021. I had no job. And I lived at home with my mom and sister in the Washington Neighborhood.

My solution was to launch my own nonprofit and change my community—a way to prove my talents and save the neighborhood.

Apple of Youth Programs

I built my own work schedule during that time with lofty goals in front of me: ten-hour days, six days a week. One sticky note read, "*They fucked up now. This life is yours.*" Another said, "Apple of youth programs in Long Beach." I wanted the impact of our youth programs to shake things up the way Apple changed technology. Changed the world. *Greatness.*

I devoured everything I could find on starting a nonprofit. I was obsessed with it. I saw it as not only changing the neighborhood but also showing the naysayers. The people who passed me up. The people who didn't respect me. The people who rejected me. The people who overlooked me or took me for granted. The people who ignored me. The people who left me hanging. I wanted them to see that this young adult from the *barrio* could get things done. Could change the game.

From all the information I gathered, I created a framework to jump-start the process. I went through the following three steps:

1. **Is there a need?** Identify if this idea is something the community really needs.
2. **Is somebody already addressing it?** Research any groups tackling the issue to see if we could support them instead of replicating efforts.
3. **How hard are you willing to work?** Figure out if this is something you can see yourself doing long-term and not just some one-and-done impulsive pipe dream—because building something real takes time.

I checked off each question mark and completed hundreds of hours of research. I used the most alarming, tangible data points as my sword in battle. One stat I pulled—after measuring the size of Long Beach—showed that the Washington Neighborhood represents around 2 percent of the city's population, yet accounts for about 10 percent of violent crime.[23] It exposed how disproportionately the neighborhood bears the ugly burden of violence. The need was real, and I had to build something strong enough to face it toe to toe.

I learned that when starting a grassroots nonprofit, forming a 501(c)(3) isn't always the best move. A 501(c)(3) gives you official nonprofit corporation status with the federal government to operate as a standalone tax-deductible agency. But it comes at a cost. Founders can end up buried in paperwork, legal fees, and red tape rather than the work in community. Instead, you could be a fiscally sponsored project that lives under the umbrella of another nonprofit that holds your funding. It's like having a big sister watch your back while out on the playground trying to make new friends. It made sense to me. The fiscal sponsor handles all those administrative tasks, including liability, insurance, permits, and billing.

Launching (Section 2)

My next move was forming a team. All my great basketball moments revolved around having a great team. I knew that if I wanted to have a strong impact, I couldn't do it alone.

The first person I approached was my friend Danny. We were in the same college society and were like-minded—maybe it was our shared Cancer sign. He was honest, kind-hearted, and ambitious, with a drive to make a real difference. On top of that, he did photography in his free time.

I pitched the idea to Danny inside the Long Beach State Student Recreation Center, or the WREC, as we called it. I broke down the makeup of the neighborhood and what I hoped to accomplish. Much convincing wasn't needed. Danny was all in. Growing up in Boyle Heights, he was very familiar with neighborhood traumas, gang violence, and inequities. He had *skin in the game*.

I knew we needed some basketball talent as well. Experts and savants of the game. So I reached out to old high school teammates. Gabe, a few years older, was someone I'd always looked up to. I remember rushing to his games after school with a couple hamburgers stuffed in my jacket pocket from the local taco shop. I hardly touched the low-quality lunch food; we called it prison food and stayed away. With my late lunch in hand, plain burgers with ketchup, I studied how Gabe controlled the game's tempo and put in extra effort. He was a consistent scorer, with the floater and three-pointer being his weapons of choice. A smaller-sized guard with a high IQ. You could tell he had devoted 10,000 hours of mastery.

At the time of starting Books & Buckets, Gabe was all in on his training and influencing platform, Quicksandmindset. He was training young athletes in the game of basketball and the journey of the mind. It was bigger than the game.

He had all the right qualities to lead the athletic development of Books & Buckets.

Gabe was a neighborhood kid out of San Pedro who knew what it was like to be counted out. He wanted to help out those who were left behind, overlooked, and underrated. Just like he was. As a high school athlete, Gabe never got the recognition he deserved. People got caught up in his size rather than his dedication to the game. He was arguably the coldest point guard walking on our campus. Gabe wanted to ensure the next generation of underdog neighborhood hoopers weren't passed up like he was. Quicksandmindset and Books & Buckets joined forces.

We also needed someone with serious playing experience—someone who had played college or pro basketball to serve as a role model for the youth. One of the few teammates I knew with a solid playing career was Travis. He was a junior when I was a freshman in high school, and all the underclassmen thought he was super cool. He was tall, standing at 6-foot-6, could dunk with ease, and had a flat-top hairstyle. Watching him throw one down for the crowd at the games on Friday night always had us hyped.

He didn't need the sales pitch. As someone who grew up on the Westside, it was real to him. Something he always wanted to do: share his talents and skills with youth who couldn't afford the high-end training programs. Travis was all in.

We were missing someone with expertise in women's basketball, as the program was meant to be co-ed. I had a teammate in the intramural league named Marlene. She was a tall, lengthy hooper with a great triple-threat sweep-through move that could leave you in the dust. She was also heart-centered and cared about the community. I pitched the idea to her after some open runs at the WREC. I remember she loved it, so much so that she told her friend Andrea about it and recruited her as well. Marlene led all the basketball fundamentals for the girls, and Andrea was a marketing expert who crafted our first-ever branding and communications campaign.

The last piece was accountability. I needed to create my own checks and balances. And there's no one more authentic and genuine than my main man and high school teammate, Mike. I asked him to serve as President of Books & Buckets to provide oversight. I needed someone to tell it like it is when things weren't going right. *Your circle has to be filled with people who keep it one hundred.* If you smelled like spaghetti and had cilantro in your teeth, Mike would tell you straight to your face. Exactly what we needed.

Your circle has to be filled with people who keep it one hundred.

We were just a bunch of early 20-something-year-olds who didn't know what we were doing.

People often ask me how I built the team at Books & Buckets, and it's simple: with people from my social circle of influence. That's why who you surround yourself with is so important. It's your social capital.

For anyone building a team to push forward a mission, consider these **ABCs of Team Building:**

    A. **Aligning Mission and Passion**
    B. **Balancing Diverse Skillsets**
    C. **Creating Camaraderie**

    A. **Aligning Mission and Passion**: You have to choose people who are passionate about the work. People who love it so much that they are willing to show up on a Saturday without blinking. This can't be taught. It doesn't matter how skilled someone is. If they don't have the fire burning in them for the cause, well then, it's a lost cause.

B. **Balancing Diverse Skillsets**: If your team is full of clones with the same skillsets and backgrounds, conflict will reign, and you'll miss unique perspectives and ideas. You need balance, like a living-breathing ecosystem. Homeostasis in action. Bring on a plethora of talent.

C. **Creating Camaraderie**: The grind can get rough—early mornings, late nights. There needs to be a level of chemistry where meetings feel like a Friday night with friends. We can't separate social time and work time when surging on an extraordinary mission. We have to integrate them. Work-life balance produces average results. I learned this from Harvard lawyer John Mathews when I asked him how he maintains a work-life balance. He said he doesn't; instead, he focuses on integration. He'll take his partner out on a date at a community event that he also has to attend for work. He stacks them. The work for Books & Buckets had to be stacked, where meeting up on the weekend felt like hanging out with friends. We'd put in the work and have a good time. Seamless.

I put down a couple thousand dollars to get Books & Buckets off the ground—covering supplies, permits, books, anything we needed to make it happen. Our entire team was made up of volunteers. They believed in our vision, ready to make an impact without a dime in return. The only funding we had was from Habitat for Humanity, which sponsored our program as part of their Washington Neighborhood Revitalization initiative.

We launched in the summer of 2021, the height of the pandemic, at the 14th Street basketball courts. Launching at the same courts I grew up on felt surreal.

We jump-started the organization with a video about how Books & Buckets came together. Danny worked his ass off putting it together—filming, directing, editing—while I wrote the storyline in the background. I learned how to craft that story from a storytelling course called *Story & Spirit* by Michael Kass. It focused on ethical storytelling, which helped me highlight the neighborhood's problems while also showcasing the community's strength and resilience.

Books & Buckets took off. People loved the story behind the mission. The local press covered our work, from the Long Beach Post to the Press-Telegram to Spectrum News. Reporter Kristen Lago even came out to interview us on the blacktop. They filmed the youth in action and interviewed one of our sixth-graders. We were rolling.

But we still needed some funding to land. The theme at the time was "We Believe." We believed in our capability to form a strong organization with sustainable programming. That belief kept us pushing forward. I'd text the phrase in our team group chat as an ever-present reminder. And that mantra really hit when we got our first grant.

The City of Long Beach awarded us $10,000 as part of their Racial Reconciliation effort following the murder of George Floyd. We were one of the few organizations doing work in the Washington Neighborhood, a community of color, and we were building youth social capital. When that grant award email came in, I ran to the living room, celebrating as if I had just hit a game-winning shot. My sister Lisa couldn't believe it, repeatedly saying, "Bro, no way. Bro, no way." I stepped out to the back of our apartments, threw on "Funeral" by Band of Horses (Excision Remix), and let the moment sink in. That moment wasn't just a small win reinforcing our belief—it was fuel to keep us going.

Youth and families trusted our program. Over 30 local youth enrolled in this brand-new program that had no credibility, run by people fresh out of college. There was no track record and no real money, but we brought high-quality, youth-led programming to the Washington Neighborhood. I knocked on every door in the neighborhood before that summer launch, with my mom helping me pass out flyers to the señoras in the community.

Once, in the midst of it all, I stepped outside onto the balcony of our apartment to contemplate a dilemma between my life and my mission. Our balcony view was Pacific Avenue, cars racing past like they're in a high-speed chase. I stood on the armrest of the wooden plank, elbows holding me up as I gazed at the road in deep introspection. I thought about the mission: bringing peace to the neighborhood. I was ready to do whatever it took to make my neighborhood a safe and healthy place, even if it meant sacrificing my own quality of life. At 25 years old, I decided that if my life served as a sacrifice for securing peace in the community, it would be a life well-lived. I wanted to become a martyr for the movement.

Building (Section 3)

We brought the program that changed my life in Lakewood to the local courts in the Washington Neighborhood, allowing youth to walk there instead of taking a long ass bus ride. That was the dream all along. Neighborhood change built on grit and naive belief.

The first Books & Buckets Youth Academy started off with three focuses: basketball skills clinics, reading discussions, and guest speakers. The skills clinics were led by Quicksandmindset, while I ran the reading discussions and coordinated guest speakers. Our first book centered on self-empowerment, healing, and meditation. Youth were assigned chapters to read before each program day's reading discussion. After that, a guest speaker from the local government, community, or basketball world would engage with the youth. I knew basketball was what brought all the youth in, but we wanted this to be bigger than the game. That's why the first hour of each program day was dedicated to academics and advocacy. All of these elements wove together the fabric of our Youth Academy.

That first summer wasn't easy. A house fire broke out right in front of us at an abandoned home where squatters lived. We had to send the youth home because the heat from the flames could be felt on the courts. Another time, someone walked around naked near the basketball courts, approaching and distracting the youth. There was no escaping the neighborhood's struggles.

There were so many moving pieces, and it was all new to me. Fortunately, we had backup.

One of the few homeowners in the neighborhood sponsored a paletero man to hand out free Popi ice cream. And a fellow Cabrillo High alum, Andy, reached out to volunteer. He played basketball, loved supporting local youth, and was an alumnus of Washington Middle School. Andy was a great addition to the team and quickly became a marketing powerhouse for us. Then came Kelly. She grew up in Central Long Beach, aka Eastside, and even owned a business in Cambodia Town. She was a hooper, too. Kelly fit right in, building strong bonds with our youth while helping scale our operational arm.

On our third program day, I invited my friend Andrew. We worked together during my time at TNP, and I wanted him to speak about community organizing. He was the best community organizer in Long Beach and had a great deal of lived experience with gang violence. He was, and still is, very well known for organizing large groups of people to march on City Council—motivated to improve their community. Andrew had even enrolled his nephew in the program. Everything fell into play just right. That day, he discussed gang violence and how to change your neighborhood. When it comes to mobilizing a community for systems change, there's none better than Andrew. His speech was so powerful that we recruited him to join our team.

We had the fresh buzz of a new program on the block. Guests from the Mayor's Office, the Congressman's Office, and multiple elected officials—School Board member Erik Miller, School Board member Dr. Juan Benitez, and State Assemblymember Patrick O'Donnell all came out to support. Assemblymember O'Donnell even jumped in for a little one-on-one game with one of our 12-year-olds, Vincent.

(Vincent playing one-on-one with State Assemblymember Patrick O'Donnell)

Summer 2021 ran for ten weeks—half at the 14th Street courts and half at the Washington Middle School gym. We secured the gym thanks to some early funding and partnerships with the school board. It was a great first run, but I knew it had to be more. I wanted more than just another direct service program. I wanted something that shook things up, something that *shifted the conditions holding long-standing problems in place*. These issues had been around way too long, and traditional programming wasn't cutting it. We had to think bigger. Go deeper. Breaking down faulty systems and reimagining the landscape. No more Band-Aids. Real solutions at the roots of the problem.

After that first summer, I was still unemployed with no income. I was a volunteer for Books & Buckets. I didn't take a dollar from the organization; quite the opposite. Starting the organization put a hole in my wallet. My volunteer role as the Executive Director was full-time hours for those early months. But I still needed to pay the bills.

Run it Back

Before I took a step up in the workforce, I took another step back. I decided to go backpacking again.

South America was next on my list. My trusty travel buddy Ed and I set off for Ecuador, Peru, and Colombia. It was amidst the shutdowns, so everything was different. There were fewer backpackers around. We got stranded at the Ecuadorian-Peruvian border in the middle of the night because they shut it all down. At airports, employees would disinfect your backpack by spraying you down without even asking. You were forced to sanitize your hands before entering, with them vigilantly watching you smooth the alcohol-drenched foam in your hands. In Peru, you had to wear two masks, and in some places, a face shield on top of that. It wasn't enough, though. We ended up getting COVID in Ecuador and had to quarantine in some hotel. Honestly, it was a fun isolation with my boy—one that helped me figure out the next step for Books & Buckets.

We spent the days watching brain-frying reality TV shows like *Love Island* and *F-boy Island*. Every night, we'd each buy a bottle of red wine and pound it while watching our shows, no cup needed. I also caught up on all my digital organizing work and started pondering how to take things to the next level. I thought about how in the Youth Academy, neighborhood kids learn how to be active change agents. They are given a formula and a platform to transform the area they call home. It's all about learning and capacity building. But what about putting those skills to the test? I wanted the youth to put the things they learned to the test on actionable neighborhood impact projects.

The idea hit me right there in quarantine: actionable neighborhood impact. Action. Youth and action. Books & Buckets Youth Action. This was upgrading our work, and I knew we needed an expert in systems change to lead it. That was Andrew.

Neighborhood Impact

After I returned from South America, I called Andrew and asked him to lead the next iteration of Books & Buckets. This time, it would focus on tangible service projects of neighborhood impact. Putting the skills they had developed over the summer to the test, tackling conditions that created problems in the community. It was like he had already heard me say this before.

"I'm down. Honestly, this couldn't have come at a better time for me. Let's go."

Serendipity.

We had no playbook, but we knew we wanted it to be great. We had no long-standing experience, but we wanted to be wise. The Youth Action program ended up being a major hit—youth-led two massive neighborhood impact projects: the Community Cleanup/Art Sculpture and the Gang Violence Prevention Panel.

Two young sisters led the Community Cleanup/Arts Sculpture, Karena and Kayleen. One was in middle school and the other in high school. With Marlene providing mentorship and guidance, they set out to do something great to address all the trash and litter in the neighborhood. The girls were tired of living in a trash-ridden environment. And they wanted the feeling of what a clean neighborhood brings to you: safety, structure, and serenity. It's hard to be proud of your *vecindario* when it's all dirty and busted.

The two sisters organized a community cleanup with the help of local volunteers. We cleaned up the surrounding 14th Street basketball courts. But we wanted it to be more meaningful, with the root cause of the problem in mind. You see, a dirty neighborhood is a symptom of a larger problem. We can clean it up, but it will just get dirty again. Instead of mopping up the water on the kitchen floor while the sink remains overflowing, we wanted to mop up the water and turn off the faucet.

The two girls came up with the idea of collecting all the trash from the cleanup and forming it into an Earth-like structure to symbolize a world full of trash. It was a powerful statement of how they saw their neighborhood and how we treat our planet. The Earth sculpture was created with the help of artists from the Long Beach Arts Council. We took that trash-fueled Earth to the City Council, where the youth spoke on the litter in the neighborhood with hopes of mobilizing a response. The art sculpture was even featured at the Arts Council's exhibit inside the Museum of Latin American Art. It wasn't just another clean-up. It was a message.

The Gang Violence Prevention Panel came next. It stemmed from the same issue that inspired the founding of Books & Buckets. Time and time again, gang violence was brought up as the number one issue youth worried about, especially for boys. Two young men, Edrick and Mario, stepped up to tackle this issue alongside Andrew. We organized the panel at Seaside Park, a notorious park in the area that is constantly tagged up by the local gang. Many youth in the neighborhood don't go to the park out of fear of being targeted. That's exactly why we chose it. We wanted to be right there where the issue was and create a safe space out of it.

I remember mentioning to Andrew, "What if something pops off? Should we ask for extra police patrols of the park?"

Andrew felt we had enough community peacekeepers to maintain a safe environment.

"I think we'll be fine. There will be enough community members who can calmly de-escalate any situation that pops off. I also ran into some local gang members while we were canvassing. They sounded in support of the event."

He was right.

The Gang Violence Prevention Panel had over 60 community members show up. It was poppin'. Our youth leader Edrick was on the panel, along with representatives from Homeboy Industries, the City's Equity Office, Californians For Justice, and the Brothers Sons Selves Coalition. Travis and youth leader Mario facilitated the conversation. They addressed the causes of gang violence, what community members could do about it, and which programs best serve gang-impacted youth.

We also used the panel as an effort to collect survey data on people's perceptions of gang activity. It was intended to gauge the magnitude of the problem and determine whether they were willing to become a catalyst to help resolve it. Andrew collected and analyzed the data to guide our long-term efforts to end gang violence. Of the community members who completed the survey:

- 96% felt the panel had a positive impact on the neighborhood
- 50% had experienced gang violence themselves or knew someone who had experienced it
- 77% felt they now know what is needed to prevent gang violence as a result of the panel

That was the first-ever gang violence prevention panel in the Washington Neighborhood.

An ironic story about that event involved one of our youth—we'll call him Anthony. He was around 15 at the time, an up-and-coming youth organizer who was helping to put the event on. He kept a lookout on the park, making sure everything ran smoothly. Anthony took pride in keeping the community safe that day.

A few months after the panel, Anthony was getting pulled into the local gang himself. We did our best to steer him away from it. We had guest speakers talk to Anthony one-on-one at the gym. We gave him rides to the program whenever we could. I introduced him to a community interventionist worker, a.k.a. peacekeeper, to hook him up with a job. I walked the neighborhood with him, discussing the ways the area has been neglected and what success could look like for our community. I even took Anthony out to eat at a fancy dinner place with an entire view of Long Beach, hoping he'd realize there's more to life than street gangs.

Nothing worked.

Anthony went from organizing a gang prevention panel to becoming part of the problem we were trying to solve. Those are the tough cases. We failed Anthony, and the gang was coming after him ferociously. They would drive to his school and wait for him to get out of class. He was in too deep. His family ended up relocating to another state to save him from the suicide mission.

Times like those were always draining. They make you frustrated. They make you question your work. You learn that you can always get better.

Sustaining (Section 4)

I was running a nonprofit, changing the neighborhood, and doing things no one had done before. Yet, I was broke and needed to make some money. I started applying to City jobs, hoping to continue my work in the neighborhood that raised me.

I applied to seven different City of Long Beach positions, advanced to the second round of interviews for two of them, and received an offer for one of them. It was for this brand-new Office of Youth Development. The person starting the office knew about my work on creating a youth development organization from scratch in an area that needed it most. They saw what Books & Buckets accomplished in a short amount of time and believed I could do it again. This time, within a government office building from the ground up.

I finally had a job again, earning over double what I made in my first full-time job. I was working on the systems and policies of youth development at a citywide level. I helped start a plethora of first-ever programs. I had hustle and heart for my job, showing up day after day, locked in, ready to put in work. I was grateful to serve the city that raised me. And in my free time, I continued to volunteer for Books & Buckets to keep my nose to the ground and connection in the streets.

Books & Buckets started thinking long-term about some of the neighborhood impact projects. Some of them would take years. The two main projects the youth brought up were renovating the 14th Street courts and building a community center.

Centro Comunitario

Around the same time Books & Buckets started, I worked on a campaign with other locals to bring a community center to the neighborhood. It's crazy that the neighborhood with the greatest need for a community center doesn't have one. Meanwhile, other neighborhoods with far fewer issues have them. It's completely upside down—like making the severely wounded gunshot victim wait in the emergency room while nurses treat a kid with a sprained ankle.

We initially campaigned to convert the burnt-down, abandoned house near the courts into a community center. We collected over 500 signatures, thanks to some local community legends, such as Martha Cota, from the grassroots organization Latinos in Action. That campaign failed, but the word got out.

City leaders heard about our campaign, with many pledging in support. During a heated mayoral race in Long Beach, we made the community center a top priority when candidate Rex Richardson rolled into the neighborhood.

Elected officials don't often visit our neighborhood. They say it's too dangerous or not worth their time, given the low voter turnout in the area. But Rex set aside the time, and we discussed the community center possibilities. Rex verbally committed to creating the center in the neighborhood, and about a year later, he delivered. The City earmarked funding to conduct a feasibility study to see where and how a center could be built.[24] It was something the Mayor had done in North Long Beach. And his Community Engagement Deputy, Montserrat Pineda—a neighborhood kid herself from the Ramona Park neighborhood—was always a strong advocate for our community.

14th Street Courts

Renovating the basketball courts was top of mind for our youth.

Through the Youth Action program, local youth put together a 14th Street Court Vision Plan, which they presented to the City Council with the guidance of Andrew. [25] About seven neighborhood kids told the Mayor and nine Councilmembers how they wanted to revitalize the basketball courts because of what it meant to them. That meeting had about 40 community members from the Washington Neighborhood. The numbers were deep, and the message was loud.

The project featured Long Beach's first-ever outdoor basketball court community mural, where youth would select what mural they wanted to be painted on the ground of the courts and help paint it with a local artist. The entire vision plan requested upgrades to the backboards, rims, fences, floors, lines, shading, seating, and even a push for a restroom in the area, as well as quality water fountains.

The Long Beach Arts Council featured a group of artists who drew up renderings of what a mural on the basketball court could look like. Our youth selected artist Tracy Negrete Allen's designs—someone who also knew the neighborhood well. With Tracy's help, those outdoor courts will go down as some of the nicest in all of Long Beach. The neighborhood with the largest caseload of trauma deserves the highest quality services to combat that trend. The future community center should follow the same example.

The 14th Street courts and community center are critical for neighborhood peace. You need as many play zones as possible to deter youngins from falling into the wrong path. Safe havens for youth are a blessing—centers, studios, playgrounds, sports fields, and any other space where young people can create, play, and explore in a welcoming, wholesome environment. That's what we were trying to create for the neighborhood. Impact that went beyond any one-and-done program. Something that lasted in perpetuity.

When Books & Buckets first launched, there was one thing I knew for sure—I wanted it to be sustainable. I wanted it to outlive any one person. If something happened to me, it would just keep plugging along.

Oftentimes, nonprofits stall without their founder because they're built around that person's identity, tangled in ego and power. I didn't want that. I wanted something truly genuine and community-led. I didn't want people to just think about me when they saw all the great work. I wanted them to think about the youth, the local parents, the directors, the volunteers, and an overarching sense that this initiative belongs to the community, not any one person. Over time, this has gradually become the case. Books & Buckets pushes forward with or without me, uplifted by a team that can autonomously operate. The dream was for the program to blossom and prosper without me behind the wheel.

Soon enough, *this was put to the test when a life-altering accident came speeding my way.*

(Ed and I in Southeast Asia's largest freshwater lake, Tonle Sap)

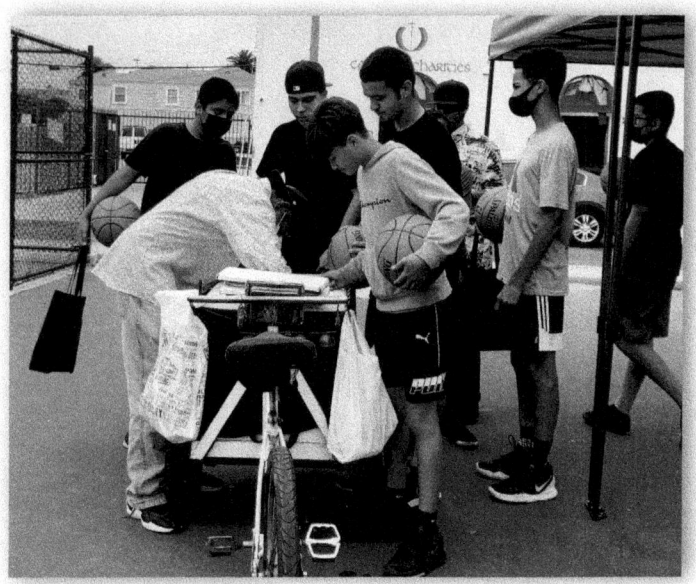

(A paletero man passing out the free ice cream sponsored by a local resident)

(The house that caught on fire during our program)

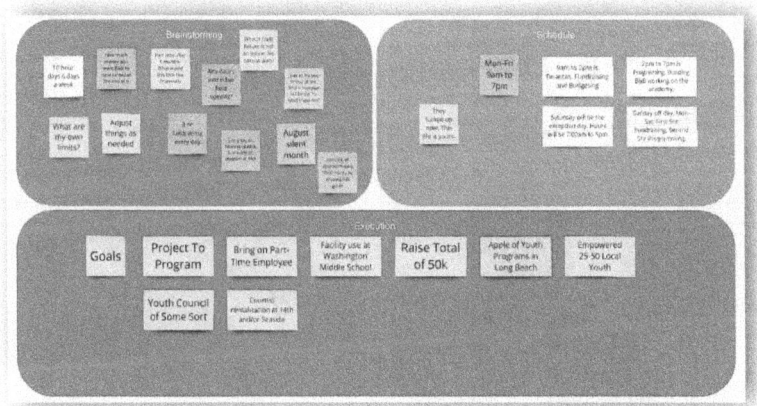
(6-month Books & Buckets plan right after becoming unemployed)

(Books & Buckets team photo at 14th Street courts: Marlene, me, Gabe, Andrea, Danny, and Travis, respectively)

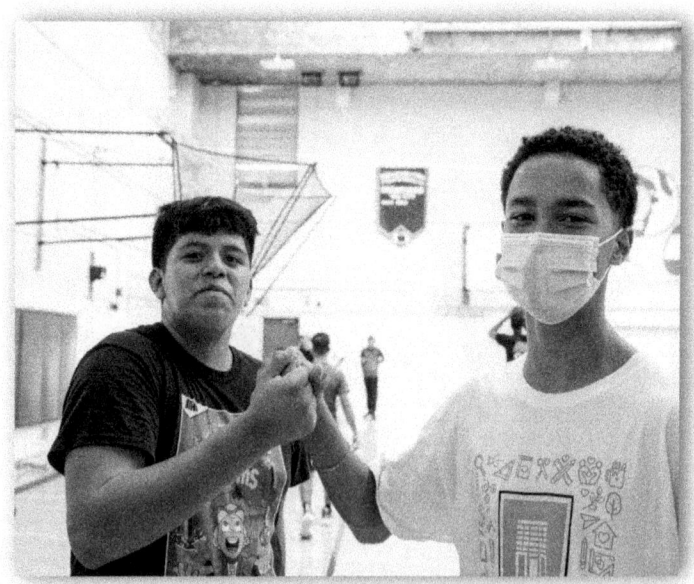

(Books & Buckets first summer youth academy at Washington Middle School)

PART III

THE TRANSFORMATION OF YOUR NEIGHBORHOOD AND THE NEIGHBORHOOD KID

NEIGHBORHOOD VICTIM

Izzy and I were riding a bike off Pacific Avenue. We were 12 years old at the time. I was on the pegs while he powered through, pedaling and pulling double the weight. We had to get across the street to get home, so he took a couple of over-the-shoulder looks to see if any cars were coming. Then he took a sharp turn to cross. The turn was so tight that our weight and my height, with me on the pegs, made us tip over and fall to the ground. Since I was elevated already on the pegs, I had some airtime once I fell off. I ended up laid out on my back in the middle of the street like someone knocked me out. Izzy called out, "Bird, you good?" I don't know why, but I just laid there for a second with my arms stretched out. I guess it took a bit to realize I was on the ground and was okay. I looked up at him. He started busting up because I was lying there like I died or sum. I finally got up, hopped back on the pegs, and we dipped out. No cars came through that entire time as we playfully dusted ourselves off. It's still a funny moment that we laugh about to this day.

We were never afraid of the cars in the streets, despite the number of close encounters. The potential of losing your life from a car just doesn't give the same fear response as gang violence, regardless of the reality.

We feared the streets with violent gangs targeting young men. We feared getting shot, stabbed, or jumped. There were streets we never walked down because we knew who lived in which apartments. And we never wanted to get caught slippin.'

But the streets full of gangs aren't the most violent aggressors in the neighborhood. Our streets full of cars are.

Deadly Corridors

In Long Beach, there are more traffic fatalities than murders. From 2021-2024, an average of around 42 traffic fatalities occurred every year, larger than the average of around 35 murders.[26] Homicides get the attention, but your commute is even more dangerous.

The Washington Neighborhood has one of the highest rates of traffic collisions and fatalities in Long Beach. If you look at the city's high-injury corridors, Central Long Beach is blasted red with recorded collisions and injuries.[27]

There are numerous factors at play. The neighborhood is densely packed in a city built for cars. Some families live three to four deep in a busted-up one-bedroom apartment. Most of these units don't have tenant parking, so the streets and alleys stay flooded with cars. Even the middle island gets used as a parking space.

On top of that, the asphalt streets have potholes that'll take your tire out. Speed bumps are nowhere to be found, and high-accident corridors lack crosswalk lights.

The political agenda doesn't prioritize traffic fatalities, often times mistakenly seeing them as inevitable accidents that can't be prevented. We've been pushing for more crosswalk safety and street lights, but the calls have gone unanswered.

Another aspect to consider is how people dealing with strains and stressors of living paycheck to paycheck, gun violence, pollution, and an area crowded by liquor stores and smoke shops might not be their best at the wheel. That anger, frustration, stress, and addiction can creep up on you in road rage.

The intersection at Pacific Avenue and 16th Street is especially notorious. I grew up off Pacific. I've collected videos and photos from the weekly accidents over the years. It's a four-lane street with an opening on 16th that includes a crosswalk with yield lights and painted lines. There are no physical speed reducers. No red light. The major momentum enemy is a deadly hill located right before the crosswalk near Washington Middle School. The hill adds nitrous to cars already speeding. I know that hill well. My boy Izzy and I used to sit on our skateboards near the school and catch it all the way down to the end of the block. The hill brought us joy growing up, something overshadowed by the door of violence it left open.

It's interesting how the Washington Neighborhood has a high number of children and youth, yet it's one of the most dangerous places to walk or ride a bike in. It should be the opposite, no? It sounds ludicrous that I even just said that statement.

The area with the highest proportion of children and youth is one of the most dangerous places to walk or ride your bike in.

It's hard to even fathom that. It's the same paradox as the community center. Shouldn't the most dangerous neighborhood in the city have the biggest and best community center to help curb the violence? This stuff isn't rocket science.

Once, there was a señora who had just finished washing her family's clothes at the local laundromat. In the neighborhood, people don't have the luxury of an in-home washer and dryer. They have to walk or drive to a laundromat and pay for their clothes to be cleaned in areas surrounded by liquor stores, smoke shops, gang violence, drug deals, illicit sex work, encampments, engine-oiled-up asphalt, and unstable conditions. Just going to the laundromat in a dangerous neighborhood is a stressor in itself. But that's not even what we're talking about here. We are talking about the walk home. The most dangerous walk home of this señora's life.

As she was crossing Pacific and 16th with her laundry basket full of clothes, she was plummeted by a speeding car, leaving her motionless on the ground, faced down with clothes scattered across the street. I have a picture of the accident that I have never shared out of respect for the family. At the time, I took it to spread awareness about the issue. But I never shared it because I later realized it wasn't for me to take. She probably had kids who were at home waiting for their mom to come back safe, with clean clothes in hand, ready to make them some food. I'm still not sure if she survived.

Thinking about that happening to my mom after the hundreds of laundry runs she did for us over the years brings pain to my stomach and tears to my eyes as I write this.

Violence tears us apart, and it has many faces: cars behaving as death machines, misguided men looking to harm others, or an environment that degrades your health. We have fought back. Or at least tried. My mom and I, along with our neighbors, have taken to the streets, blocking a major highway with just twenty people demanding peace.[28] Also, we've stood up for our neighbor, who sells corn and raspados to the local residents, when two young men assaulted him with a gun to secure a quick lick.[29] Sometimes these uprisings make you feel like you are making an impact. Other times, you are overcome with frustration from the constant battles.

There are so many pitfalls of problems in the neighborhood. You look right—there's a speeding car about to run you over. You look left—young men are shooting at each other. You look ahead—someone is living on the streets with a mental illness, yelling at you, ready to steal your dog (true story). You look back—people are pulling out guns and shooting at the ground over an argument about a parking spot (true story). You look down—dirt and filth cover the corners, with alleys drowning in mattresses and cockroach-infested cabinets. You look up—pollutants, smoke, and air particles chip away at your health and shorten your lifespan. *You look inward, and all you want to do is leave the neighborhood that raised you by whatever means necessary.*

Whatever way you look at it, it's a battle out there.

Desite my efforts to win those battles, I took my Ls. The Pacific and 16th intersection was well known to me and Izzy. When I was about 13, we were crossing it to go play basketball. A car we had thought was slowing down ended up speeding right through us, clipping our shirts and leaving us feeling the wind of its wake. We got lucky that time.

Another time, I was beaming around on my skateboard with my boys. We'd just finished crossing that deadly intersection, now riding past a nearby alley, when a car speared me in my hip out of nowhere like WWE star Dave Bautista in a heavyweight championship match. I was sent flying into the street while the skateboard kept rolling along. My boys stopped riding after they heard the tires screeching to a stop, realizing I'd just gotten slept. A little busted up, but I was alright. The man jumped out of his car while his family stayed inside. You could tell he was scared of what might happen to him. He didn't speak English, so I responded in Spanish, told him not to worry about it, picked up my board, and kept riding.

That was strike two for me. *On Feb 3, 2023, I struck out.*

Struck Out

It was a Saturday night, another night on the town to let loose and hang with the boys. I was dropped off in front of my apartment after going to an underground comedy show. Some of the details of the night are still fuzzy. I don't remember exactly what led to what, but a few moments stand out.

I was walking across Pacific and 16th after pressing the walking yield light. There was a car down the road that I thought would stop as I walked across, taking ownership of the pedestrian right-of-way. But the headlights kept coming—brighter and brighter at a constant speed. I assumed the car would swerve out of the way or come to a screeching stop soon. Unfortunately, the driver did neither.

There's a split-second moment that's enough time for me to realize I was fucked, but not enough time for me to do anything about it. Not even enough time to move out of the way, brace myself, or scream.

Next thing I know, I'm in a hospital bed with fentanyl in my IV, numbing the pain. My mom and sisters are to my left, their faces filled with anguish. A police officer to my right, firing off questions. Blood covers my head. Scabs from the street cling to the left side of my face. Clothes drenched in crusted, dried blood. My right leg is destroyed. Open wounds cover my body from top to bottom—carved in from skidding across the street.

My oldest sister takes a look at the left side of my face and says, "This looks like permanent damage. You might be disfigured."

I wish she hadn't said that. A sudden rush of anxiety clenches my stomach with a death grip.

The police officer pressed me for answers while I was still drugged up on fentanyl, asking why I was crossing the street. Someone on the street heard the crash of a speeding 2,000-pound metal moving object tackling my 170-pound human frame. They called 911, and the paramedics took me to the nearest hospital. Saint Mary's, once again.

A crowd had gathered at the crash site, watching as I screamed in pain. Someone even recorded it and posted the video on the neighborhood social media platform, NextDoor. My mom and sisters watched the video while we were in the hospital. I wish they hadn't.

My sister got the post taken down. And I now have that video.

It was a hit-and-run.[30] The driver was nowhere to be found. Witnesses reported that it was a red car, and after it hit me, the car slowed down for a second before speeding off. They left me for dead.

At the hospital, the diagnosis was rough—I dislocated my right knee, tore my ACL, PCL, MCL, and lateral meniscus, broke my tibia, and my ear was nearly ripped off the side of my head from skidding across the asphalt. It was like the board game, *Operation*. They had to put me back together. My head was covered in wounds, but miraculously, no concussions. Just scabs and bruises from the fall.

Oh, and my fire was put out.

The trauma surgeon said my knee was so demolished that they may have to amputate it to prevent blood flow from being cut off. That one scared the hell out of me. The doctor made us choose: potential leg amputation or drill in this medieval thing called an external fixator. It *fixes* bones by drilling into them while sitting *externally* outside the skin. I had never heard of it. But come to find out, I had seen it in the movies. He guaranteed us the external fixator would save my leg.

The family left the decision solely up to me. "Whatever you think is best," I remember them saying. I had to make that call after being destroyed by that car and then drugged up on fentanyl. I couldn't even imagine losing my leg and the ability to play basketball on two feet. So I chose the fixator. No research or evidence behind a major life decision. I wish I had at least a few hours to think it through. It would've been a great time to have my dad there to lean on for words of wisdom.

They drilled four holes into my leg, two in my upper thigh and two in my shin. Metal poles stuck out from each of the holes, connected by a rectangular cage that kept them all in place. It was a metal prison around my leg, with four open wounds. I had to wear it for a month. It prevented me from bending my leg and gave the knee time to regain some stability. That was my first surgery. The second was fixing my ear.

A plastic surgeon was called into the trauma room. Her name was Dr. Stafford, and she was an angel. Tall, in her 50s, with glasses that made her appear as an avid reader. She took a look at how much skin from my ear could be salvaged. She said about 60 percent of the ear was removed from the left side of my face. Still, she seemed hopeful.

"I'm going to get it back together," she said with her hand resting on my good leg. That one gesture brought me a sigh of relief and an inch of hope.

I went under again, and she pieced it together bit by bit. The best she could.

By the second surgery, I was about a week into my hospital stay. My neighbors down the hall were people who lived on the streets or were struggling with mental illness. The hallways were full of screams, and the nurses looked like they hated being there, as if it was just a stop, not a stay. It for sure didn't feel like a place where I was going to recover. They woke me up every hour or so to check my vital signs, insert a new IV, or clean my room. It was torture being there.

Every night, I'd watch the movie *Bleed For This* on my phone. I watched it with my dad in the theatre when it first came out. It tells the story of Vinny Pazienza, a famous boxer who survived a horrible car accident and was given an external fixator on his head to heal his spine. His circle of family and friends treated him like he'd died. But he refused to accept the prognosis and believed he could heal. Vinny even lifted weights with those metal poles screwed into his skull and the cage around his head. Despite everyone counting him out, he eventually came back from the injury and fought again.

That movie helped put me to sleep every night in the hospital.

The hardest times were in the middle of the night. No family. No friends. Just you, your injury, and *your sorrow*. I'd wake up in the middle of the night, hoping it was all just a bad dream. Once I felt the scratchy hospital sheets, heard the sound of the monitors and the screams down the hall, and felt the isolation of the sanitizing hospital room, I'd painfully realize it wasn't a dream. I'd start breaking down, crying hysterically until I fell asleep again.

While I was barely hanging on to my energy and fire, the community was waiting for a mission. My mom told me they were fired up and ready to move at my command. They were ready to protest and do whatever I asked to make our streets safer. We could have rolled deep, 50+ community members motivated by their fallen comrade. It would've made some noise. But I waved them off, asking them to stand down.

I let Mom know that I didn't want to fight. I just wanted to heal. But looking back, I wish they had mobilized without me, or despite me.

Ironically, a couple of days after my accident, I was set to go to City Council to be recognized as a Dr. Martin Luther King Jr. Peacemaker Awardee for my work with gang-impacted youth in the Washington Neighborhood. I was set to deliver a speech to the Mayor, City Council, and community. The award was presented by Councilwoman Dr. Suely Saro from the sixth district as a moment to celebrate the work we accomplished in Central Long Beach. Instead of attending the meeting, I was stuck on the hopeless hospital bed. So I asked my mom to represent.

She accepted the award and delivered a speech that I had written. When she reached the part about me in the hospital having surgeries, she started crying. I watched from my Mac laptop, resting beside half-eaten hospital food and my sister Lisa and Aunt Deby on my side. I was so proud of her up there, accent and all.

After the ceremony, she rushed back to my hospital bed and apologized for crying.

It's crazy how people apologize after crying like it's something to be sorry for. How quickly we give people tissues to clean up their tears rather than letting them flow in their beautiful fall. Our relationships with emotions are all messed up. Instead of being friends with our emotions and allowing them to enter our home with an invitation to open our fridge and grab something to eat, we ostracize them. We deem them as bad, so we put up a barbed wire fence with an electric shock to keep them away. But emotions come and go, and we should see them as a natural process of *energy in motion* (e-motion) and expression. Let their motion pass.

My mom told me that a group of community members attended the City Council meeting and then headed straight to the hospital, fired up and ready to make something happen. They wanted to visit me, but my room had a guest limit. They also wanted to make some noise about Pacific and 16th, protesting by blocking traffic to force attention to the problem. I didn't want that, though. I was ashamed of the whole thing and holistically weak from being run over by that car and my neighborhood. I knew the stress of fighting back would've slowed my healing.

All I wanted was a way out of my situation. My biggest battle was no longer bringing peace to the neighborhood; it was my need to rejuvenate and bring peace to my soul.

Mom's Unanswered Calls

I can only imagine how my mom felt seeing her son so weak and beaten up. It especially hit hard for her because she had fought for years to make that intersection safer. She spoke out numerous times, but her calls for help went unanswered.

About a year *before* my accident in April 2022, my mom was on KTLA Channel 5 News speaking out about a crash that happened at the same intersection.

A car ran over a mother and her young daughter while they were on their way to school that morning. It was a whole scene. Mom rushed outside and joined fellow neighbors in an effort to find out what was going on. Every time there's an accident, there's a mayhem of people rushing to see if everyone's OK.

You can see my mom on the news, both responding to the incident while the mother and daughter were being hauled off by paramedics, and the next day, where a community protest erupted. Channel 5 interviewed my mom while she was holding up a sign. "We need the City...fix this." It was another call for help.

She saw her community members, time and time again, victimized by the violent acts of this intersection. She was fed up.

Her time as a spectator turned into a grieving mother, a year later, when she got a call about her son being run over at the same place she had repeatedly begged the City of Long Beach to fix.

Home To Heal

My time in the hospital felt like months. It felt like my injuries weren't healing in there. Both the injuries on my body and the injuries to my spirit. I knew I had to make it out of the hospital if I was going to get better.

I talked to my sister Lisa about going home to see what she thought. I even asked if I could stay with her because she had a big TV with all the streaming sites. I also didn't want to be home alone. Staying with her meant being around more people, and spared her the burden of driving back and forth to visit me at my mom's.

The next time another doctor walked in (I had about ten doctors working on my case), I asked about my discharge date. The doctor hesitated, as if he was caught off guard, filtering through his papers to buy himself time to form a response. I told him I was ready—that I needed to go home to get better. I begged that doctor to set me free.

You can't just get up and leave whenever you want. There are procedures you have to learn to take care of yourself. And if you leave without official approval, your insurance might refuse to pay for medical bills.

He felt my emotions, saw the journey in my eyes, and hesitantly agreed to write the papers for my release. After he said, "OK, we'll get you sent home then," I wanted to start bawling crying. I held it in. Only one large tear made it out of the ether, slowly sliding down my right cheek.

Lisa noticed and asked me what was wrong. The tear confused her because it was good news. I didn't respond. I stared ahead like I was locked in a staring contest with the end of the room, knowing that catching eye contact with my sister's eyes of love and care would relinquish the avalanche of emotions that wanted to break free. Looking back, I wish I had just started crying and letting it all out. I wish I had unleashed the emotions through authentic expression. It was a mix of everything: sadness from the entire trauma of the accident, desperation from being at the hospital, and the joy of relief to go home. A weird cocktail of emotions. It felt like both the ending and the beginning of my next step towards healing the body and soul of this neighborhood kid.

I lived on my sister's couch for a while. Mom and sis brought me food and water. A physical therapist frequented the home to help me adjust, teaching me how to use the bathroom and sleep with less pain. They gave me a bottle of oxycodone to help numb the pain. I only got up to wash myself or use the restroom. I started with a walker, making my way through the hallways of the home, but after a week, I switched to crutches. I felt they would challenge my body and mind more. Watching *Bleed for This* stuck with me—not to deny what I was going through, but to push myself in a way that felt like I was progressing. Every move I made was either making me better or making me worse. It was a mental battle against feeling stuck in a state I was drowning in. I needed to remind myself that my body and mind were capable of transcending, healing, and blossoming into a new reality. I didn't want to play the victim. I was aligning the trillions of cells in me with the best possible chances for a comeback.

A couple weeks after being released from the hospital, I ended up right back in there. One of the holes in my leg got infected—something that can easily happen when an open wound is exposed with a metal pole sticking out. It's like getting stabbed and just leaving the knife in. It's a painful, gruesome experience cleaning those wound sites. Moving around was a nightmare due to the fear of ripping open more skin. It's a mental battle just looking at the open holes in your leg. I had never seen anything like it. My skin was begging to close up, but every move slightly increased the size of the holes.

This return visit to the emergency room was awful. First, some big doctor, over six feet and 300 pounds, cleaned my wound sites without anesthesia by pushing my skin up and down the four poles. It was excruciating pain. Even my mom leaned back, screaming as if she was the one being treated, "Ouuuuucccchhhh!" Her face twisted with a sour grimace like she couldn't watch. I nearly broke the metal handles of the hospital bed trying to endure the pain. Then

I got an allergic reaction from the antibiotics, Red Man's Syndrome, where I just wanted to scratch off my skin until I bled.

It was rough being back in the hospital for something that got worse when I was supposed to be getting better. But *healing journeys aren't linear.*

My third surgery was scheduled to take off the external fixator a month after they put it on. Then, a fourth, to undergo a multi-ligamentous knee reconstruction allograft: using ligaments from a dead body to replace the ones that were torn. Four surgeries in four months. After each surgery, it was back to ground zero again. I would be lying if I said it wasn't discouraging to undergo damage, heal, rehab, get better, get worse again, then get better again, and repeat. Starting from scratch is one thing. Starting from ground zero four separate times was mentally debilitating.

My friend Jason visited me every Friday during that time. Friendships are tested in the darkest times. We'd watch Laker games or *Love Island* when he visited. That was the highlight of my week—lying on a couch next to Jason, chopping it up like old times, acting like being stuck there with a cage around my leg, piercing my skin and bones, wasn't my reality for those couple of hours. Those were the most exciting moments when life revolved around a couch 24 hours a day. I'd wake up laid up on the couch, watch TV laid up on the couch, and go to sleep laid up on the couch. All in the same spot. That couch was tired of me.

We sometimes take this free life full of hangouts and events for granted. *It feels so good to move about the world.*

I had a long road of recovery ahead of me. *I knew that the lowest point of my life would require my greatest point.* The movie *Bleed for This* inspired me to start lifting weights while stuck on the couch. My mom and sister would see me on the edge of the sofa, lifting a dumbbell like I was trying to push the wrath of life up from under me.

During recovery, I had a couple of visits from people involved with Books & Buckets. Andrew came by with a signed basketball that all the youth wrote messages on. Another was a Books & Buckets volunteer, Erick, who brought over Vitamin Water as a gift. He didn't have to visit me, especially since he had just started sponsoring the program, but I was grateful he did. You see who the real ones are when you're on a low one.

He asked, "So what's going to happen with Books & Buckets now that you are out? Is that it? Or.....?" He thought maybe it would disappear without me or take a break. However, the sustainability plan started from the jump of launching the nonprofit. I told him, "It's going to keep going because this has always been bigger than me. It's about the neighborhood."

Shortly before the accident, I onboarded our first-ever part-time employee to serve as a project coordinator. There was no better time for that position to step up and take charge. During my absence, everyone, from employees to contractors, volunteers, and youth participants, stepped up their game. Neighborhood kids showing support for this neighborhood kid.

Naivete

While lying on that couch, growing tired of answering hundreds of "How are you doing?" messages, I came across a random YouTube video that leveled up my recovery process. It was some rich dude spending millions to become 18 again. His name was Bryan Johnson. He launched a project called Blueprint, where he planned to measure all his organs and reverse his biological age—to the point of ending death. *Infinite horizons.* That's what he was going for.

Such a ridiculous goal, right? I remember thinking, *How naive can he be to think that's even possible?*

But what reeled me in was how openly he shared his $2 million dollar protocol: how he was eating, sleeping, exercising, supplementing, living, and just about everything he was doing to rejuvenate the human body. The public science experiment of the protocol was mission-driven. And I thought, *Damn, if this stuff is rejuvenating his body and making him young again, it sure as hell should help rejuvenate mine and help me get back to me.*

If he were that naive to think he could conquer death, then I could be a bit naive to think I can heal from these injuries and come back better than ever. Naivete is a concept I have always contemplated. My career has focused on the ecosystem of youth development, and I once gave a speech to about 100 City employees at a livability summit unpacking the concept of naivete that we associate with young people. Youth always get the wrap of how naive they are. And it's true. They are naive because they have less experience of what the world is really like sometimes. But I don't always view that as a drawback. There's a reason why so much artistry and new ideas come from youth. They have the beginner's mind, open to endless possibilities. Naivete can be a powerful tool. We should all be a bit more naive, dreaming bigger, becoming more creative, and developing ingenious solutions.

It was my turn to be naive about my bleak recovery process. I decided to implement my own version of the Blueprint protocol, shooting for an unheard-of comeback. I began devouring the information on the Blueprint website and rewatched his videos countless times. I was in hyper-focused mode, a state of intense information download. I gathered everything I could find and then started writing out my own protocol.

It started off with baby steps—asking my mom to include more vegetables in my meals or making sure I got enough sleep. With each little win, I felt something come back to me. Like what belonged to me. My agency. Not my victimhood.

My responsibility was to make decisions that got me out of my physical and mental mess. That shift put me on a compounded improvement curve, one brick at a time.

Focus on the brick, not the wall. An analogy I picked up from the artist Will Smith. He was helping his dad build a wall through the slow process of brick-laying. As a young boy, he was overwhelmed by the thought of how long it would take to build the wall. He cried, moaned, and complained over how endless the process felt. Will's dad snapped him out of thinking about the demoralizing length of the entire endeavor and made him focus on laying down each brick, as best as he could. Next thing you know, brick by brick, he built that wall. Moment by moment, I would heal my injuries.

After my third surgery, I moved back to my mom's place. Living at my sister's place gave me the anonymity I needed—nobody knew me in her condos. It wasn't like the packed housing complex I grew up in, where everybody knew your business. I was trying to avoid people when I had that external fixator on.

When I was readmitted to the hospital after the wound sites got infected, I remember passing through the hospital door with everyone staring. People would stop in their tracks when they saw me. I heard, "Eww, what is that?" and "Omg, that looks like it hurts." I tried to ignore the reactions, but they often infuriated me.

Removing that medieval external fixator stripped away the shame that came with it. And with that cage off, it was time to return to my childhood home, where the window overlooked the crosswalk at the intersection of Pacific and 16th.

The Chance

It was different being back. I knew it when, in the middle of the night, my mom came rushing to my room, knocking on the door in a panic.

"Mijo, es muy urgente" (Son, it's very urgent).

Slowly, through aches and pains, I made my way to the door with the help of my crutches. I asked what was wrong. She told me a fifteen-year-old young man was hit by a car off Pacific between 15th and 14th, near where I was hit.

She said he had been walking home from playing football, and in the mix of things, a car ran him over. She was fired up, angry at what happened. She regretted not protesting for me.

"Me arrepiento que no hicimos nada después de lo que te pasó" (I regret not doing anything after what happened to you).

Frustration tightened my face—eyebrows squinting, eyes lowering, head nodding, hands upward and outward lifting in despair, "Qué quieres que yo haga" (What do you want me to do?).

"No soy Superman, véame" (I'm not Superman, look at me).

In a cast, a brace, and a headband holding my surgically repaired ear in place, *I was over it.*

I was over trying to "save" the neighborhood. Over sacrificing myself for peace. Over making myself a martyr for the neighborhood to prosper. My self-sacrifice for the sake of the neighborhood was similar to the suicide mission that gang members sign up for. They die for the set. I was ready to die for the mission. But surviving an accident that could've ended my life made me realize: I can't continue this kamikaze mission.

I laid back in my bed as my mom walked away, rejected and deflated at a time when she sought guidance from her neighborhood kid. The old me would've gone full-on Optimus Prime Autobot rollout: unite the community, spread awareness about the incident, text a few politicians, and even go visit the young man in the hospital. I would've joined my mom in arms and helped with the difficult tasks like technology, flyers, funding, whatever was needed.

Instead, I was beaten down. Energy dimmed. Fire extinguished. I only wanted to recover. I didn't want to fight no more.*

Sometimes the problems you are trying to address will come after you. They hunt you down. Wear you out. Make you tap and beg for mercy. That's how they stop you from solving them. Sometimes, they even take you out. This happened to the artist Nipsey Hussle. He was gunned down while trying to repair the damage done to his community. Nipsey bought the local business plaza in his childhood neighborhood and opened up mission-driven stores. He hired locals to raise the value of his neighborhood. He remodeled a local basketball court at an elementary school. He was even planning to buy entire blocks in the neighborhood to renovate the homes and give them back to the community. Despite all that, he was taken out by someone he grew up with.

Trying to put out fires might leave you burnt.

The Pacific Avenue corridor is just as dangerous as the night I was hit. The City added an extra yield light sign in the middle of Pacific Avenue, but even that has been hit by cars speeding through the runway. There is a plan to transform the Pacific Avenue track, but not until 2028.

The irony of it all was how I went to physical therapy in Santa Monica at a high-end place for athletes called Elite OrthoSport. Right outside their building on Wilshire, they also have yield intersections. But they are so much safer. The roads have bumps that drivers can feel and hear before reaching the intersection. The paint on the asphalt is clear. The islands in the middle make it feel like the City cares about you.

The Pacific and 16th intersection was even used as an example of violence in the city during a livability summit.

Myself and about 20 City employees toured the crosswalk in 2022, discussing how unconducive it was to building a livable environment. The realities were apparent both inside the government and outside in the community.

If the Mayor of Long Beach and the City Manager made that intersection a top priority, solutions would be rolled out with no excuses. But it's not a top priority. At least not yet. We have to pressure them to make those changes.

We have to make communities feel like we care about them. When someone gets hurt, we mobilize and do something about it. I hope the neighborhood continues to urge politicians to get these changes done. It's our responsibility to hold people accountable to the communities they represent. If the community doesn't bring issues to the forefront, they'll get neglected and diluted amongst other issues competing for legislative attention.

Even as a victim of this problem, I knew I was still a part of the solution. For my neighborhood, and for myself. I didn't fall for the trap of victimhood. It's not your fault when you are hit by the same issues you are trying to address. You are not to blame. *But if you get a second chance at life, it's your responsibility to pull yourself out of it. To learn from it. To grow and level up as a human.*

I was grateful for the chance at healing and getting back to me. I didn't die. My brain was ok. There was a chance to rejuvenate my vessel. That chance filled me with joy and inspiration.

You can't control what happens to you, but you sure as hell can take charge over your response. It's your responsibility to bounce back and create a new reality based on new circumstances. You are the creator of your life trajectory. Don't wait for external elements to pull you out of a pool you don't know how to swim in. Find a way to paddle back, kick across, and reach a ledge that you can propel yourself up from.

Look inward. Propel upward. *Find a way to bounce back.*

(Protesting on Pacific Ave in 2021 to bring awareness to the violence in our community)

(My mom protesting the violent intersection of Pacific Ave and 16th Street a year before I was hit)

(My mom delivering the award speech while I was in the hospital)

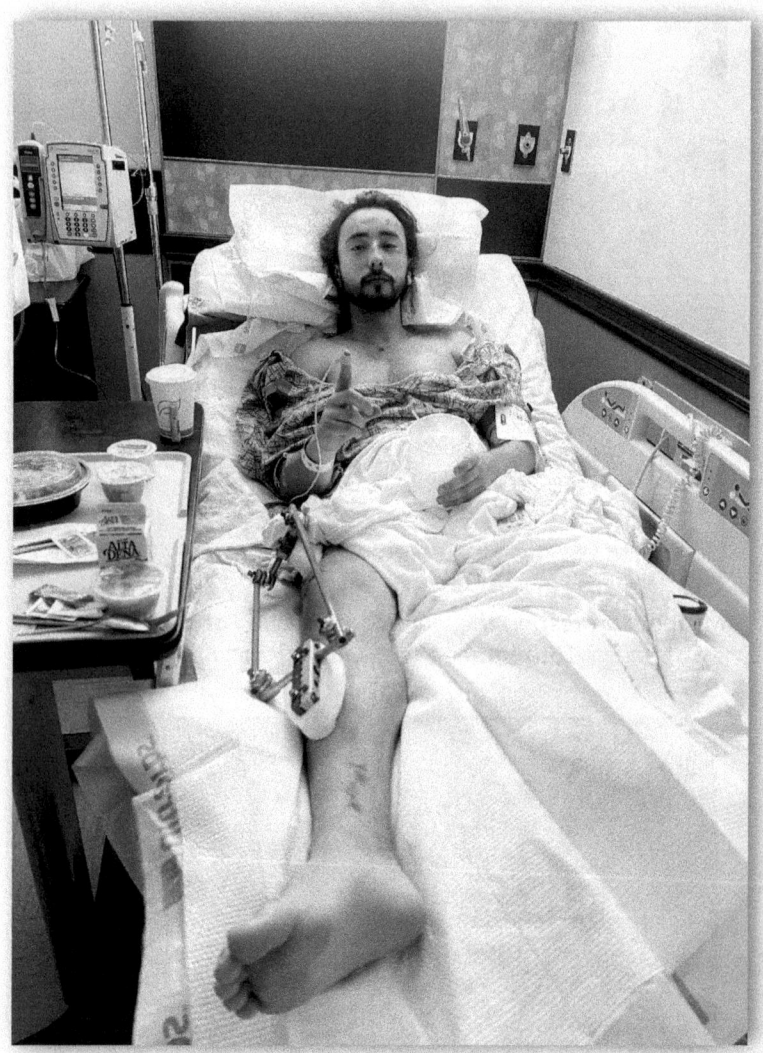

(In the hospital bed, barely hanging on to my will and pride for a better neighborhood)

NEIGHBORHOOD BOUNCEBACK

I was 25 years old when that accident hit. Prime of my life. Moving mountains in the community. Putting in work for the City. Going out dancing with friends. Talking to pretty girls. Then it all changed overnight.

I went straight to the bottom. Physical health at the bottom. Social life at the bottom. Mental health at the bottom. I wasn't interacting with much of anyone except my mom, sister, and my boy Jason.

I've been at the bottom before: growing up poor, getting evicted, losing the game of basketball, struggling with severe acne, and losing my Dad. I knew the bottom well. The bottom knew me. The bottom is like seeing a trauma surgeon in the emergency room. You never want to see them, but you're grateful they're there because you should start getting better now.

This bottom was cut from a different cloth. This bottom might've been the deepest, darkest bottom I've ever been thrown into. It's mentally degrading when someone has to wipe your ass in the hospital. When your family has to do everything for you while you lie bedridden for months. I needed a bounceback of astronomical proportions.

The Process

I felt like I was reborn when I started my recovery journey. Before the accident, I had long hair with blonde highlights. In the hospital, my sister Lisa and a physical therapist shaved my head. The hair was knotted and tangled in dried blood. There was no saving it. I also didn't have the strength to maintain long hair. So they gave me the Dwayne The Rock Johnson look. Losing my hair reminded me of Samson the Great. His strength was in his hair. After they cut it, he lost his powers, and his enemies captured him. It symbolized the strength I lost from being run over. I wasn't the same person, literally slowly deteriorating. All my muscles were atrophying due to lack of use. They were just vanishing.

Recovery was long and arduous—like writing a book. Every little exercise was a sentence added to the story. You had to win each sentence. You couldn't get caught up in the never-ending document. If I started thinking about how long recovery would take, a year or two, I'd get overwhelmed and exhausted from thinking about it.

Early rehab was boring. It wasn't the fun, run-and-jump type. It was slow work, getting my knee moving again, bending it back, and straightening it out. Having a knee locked straight for a month, pinned in place by the external fixator, created immovable stiffness. Increasing range of motion was like fighting with a rusty bathroom faucet that hadn't been used for years—back and forth cranking to break up the rusty gunk.

There were so many dull moments during that rehab era. It left me with more time to train my mind than my leg, a battle proving to be just as hard.

I captured my thoughts throughout the journey. Poems, quotes, stories, and sayings I wrote that kept me going:

Recovery Journal

Value Regular Life

Value the car rides. Value going for a walk in the park. Value a drive down memory lane. Value pulling up to a fast-food place. Value the normal, everyday things because something can hit you and take that away. It has been taken away from me, but I'm so grateful that it is only temporary. I am not done. I will make a full comeback. I will get my life back. My bounce back. My will back. I will. I value those things. And they will return.

May 27, 2023 (after my fourth surgery): I notice my head kind of going in because of how I'm back to ground zero, starting over again, and not knowing exactly how long it will be.

May 29, 2023: My mom said something where she was confused about which surgery I was talking about because there have been so many.

June 2, 2023: I'm still in that mental and emotional mess. If it keeps hitting me, I'm going to do that neurocycle. Later tonight, I thought about being on this final lap of the trenches. The last lap in the race is the hardest, and pushing through this one is where the greatness is at. Right here. This will be your defining moment. Do you fold?

June 8, 2023: I walked to 14th Street Park Sanctuary. Crutches and all. What's crazy is I wasn't sure about it. I didn't know if I would make it or if it was even a good idea. But it was amazing. I felt strong. I caught the sunset. The wind was hitting, a little chilly. So grateful to be outside man. I saw three people I knew.

June 10, 2023: I figured out that getting out in nature and having social interaction are major keys. Those are the two recipes for getting my mind and emotions right because I was going through it at one point man. I also went on a date today. Flexion is around 100 degrees now. Need to keep pounding. I will get my flexion and extension back. Quad is probably at 20% firing.

July 9, 2023: I stood up in the shower, the first time in over 5 months. Damn, it felt good. My leg feels strong. Just getting my mobility back now. They really, really fucked up. The thought of almost losing my leg fuels me to push harder during the pain of flexion. This is my last week with the full-on brace. I walked a lot today, and even went grocery shopping. First time since surgery. It feels so good to be back. Let's go man fuck. Putting my life back together so I can take this to the next level and really enjoy it.

I want this to end

I want this to end. I want this to end. It's going to end man. It's going to end man. What if it never ends? It's going to end. I miss my Dad. I wish he would hold on to some of this. I wish I could give him some of this. I wish he could hold some of this weight. I wish he could go through this with me. I miss my Dad. I want this to end. I want my Dad. (I wrote this while crying in the car listening to Kids by MGMT.)

Fighting for Me

I feel like I am fighting for my life. Fighting for ME. For who I was. For what I can do. But at the same time, that person is dead. There's no going back. I have to reform, rebrand, be reborn. I have never been so locked in before. I had no choice. I've never been so low before, too, the deepest darkest place of my life. I had to pull out another level in me. One I didn't know I had. I had to bring back that inner monster that I had when I was a kid, just tryin' to....

Poem to my External Fixator

Them poles, them poles built me tough
Them poles, them poles built me rough
Them poles, them poles built me UP!

Inner Monster

The hardest 6 months of my life, and yet, the best 6 months of my life. The best, as in the best of me. The best of who I am. The best of digging deep. Falling in the trenches once again, and crawling out the trenches in the end. Pulling out that inner monster that I created during the rough times of childhood and asking him to help pull me out of this one, too.

They Must've Forgot

Several people would ask me: "So is that it?" "Will you always walk with a limp?" "Is that it for basketball?" "Will you always have a brace?"

It fired me up. They must've forgot.

Fell Off Poem

They said I fell off. Never to be normal again.

I agreed.

They ran me over. Left me for dead. I was laid out in my own blood. On my own street. In front of my own apartment. In my own neighborhood. In my own city.

They said I might lose my leg. I said that's not an option. They put me back together like a puzzle piece, cause I had more in me, more to keep, more to release.

Things People Said to Me

"There's a chance we have to amputate."
"He'll never be the same."
"Your leg will never be normal."
"Your knee will always be stiff."
"This was a bad injury."
"Your mobility may never come back."
They fired me up, man. I love that type of stuff cause it fuels the tank.

Fear of No Greatness

How are you going to be afraid of not getting there if you already got there? The greatness is in the process, not the result. The greatness of the result is nothing without the greatness of the process. The greatness of the process is greatness regardless of the result. You are here. You got the greatness. This process is the greatness. Greatness is when you are down in the dumps, tired, ready to call it quits, but then you push through and pull yourself out of it. That's greatness. When you think you can't do this anymore, and then you just do it.

My body was run over by a car, but my spirit wasn't.

I used all that time to create. Created mantras that kept me going. Created sayings that kept me focused. Every few steps forward, followed by a step back, then a couple more forward.

I needed to bounce back in a way that transcended everything I went through. I wanted to regain the love I had for my neighborhood while gaining a new outlook on life.

Trust in Yo Self

One thought kept circling my mind during recovery—what I'd tell the neighborhood kids when I got back in the gym. I replayed the scenario in my head over and over again. It added fuel to the tank when I was running on empty.

One theme stuck with me: "Trust in Yo Self." I had to trust in myself. Trust that I could heal. Trust that I could play basketball again. Trust that life wouldn't just be recovery and couch all day.

I had to trust myself because so many doctors gave a negative prognosis. I had to trust in my ability to pull myself out of that situation. To believe in healing beyond what was imaginable. I had to heal to where doctors couldn't believe it. Something that wasn't realistic. Unrealistic naivete, just how young people move about the world.

So, I made a playlist called *Trust in Yo Self*—with some of the most motivational songs I could find.

Trust in Yo Self Playlist

- *Genesis* – Ruelle
- *Falling* – Asher
- *Too Dry To Cry* – Willis Earl Beal (*Bleed for This*)
- *Killing in the Name* – Rage Against the Machine
- *Divenire* – Ludovico Einaudi
- *First to Love* – Maia Friedman (*I listened to this on my first drive home from the hospital.*)
- *Sail* – AWOLNATION
- *Grinding All My Life* – Nipsey Hussle
- *Patiently Waiting* – 50 Cent
- *Deliverance* – Rationale
- *Start from Scratch* – The Game
- *It's a Process* – Michael Danna
- *Ketchup* – Lil Snupe
- *Y Sigues Siendo Tu* – Grupo Marca/Arriesgado (*I sometimes need simpen music to fire me up.*)
- *Can't Stop* – Red Hot Chili Peppers
- *Living Life, In The Night* – Cheriimoya & Sierra Kidd (*from the Kung Fu Panda TikTok*)

I listened to these songs religiously. This playlist DJed every rehab session on repeat. It was my ritual.

The Speech

I made it back to the gym at Books & Buckets a few months after the accident, rocking a leg brace and a beanie to cover up my surgically repaired ear. I was still waiting on my fourth and final surgery to complete the knee reconstruction. At that moment, I was missing an ACL, PCL, MCL, and a meniscus.

I sat down on a chair to give my knee a break and to tell them what I knew they were all waiting for. Everyone in the gym wanted to know what the fuck happened. What was my dumbass doing? How did I get hit? What damage was done? I walked them through the night of the accident, at least what I could remember. But I didn't want the whole speech to be about my hardship or how much it sucked.

So I dialed in something worth their attention: *trusting in yourself*. I knew those young people would face battles in their own lives, which would require an anchor to hold them steady through the storm. I let them know that when their back's against the wall, when they're at their lowest, they can always still trust in their power to *bounce back*. A state like they've never experienced before. An evolution.

I learned the "back against the wall" mentality from The Rock's speech to the Los Angeles Lakers.[31] The Rock said every day his back is up against the wall, and there is nowhere to go but forward. It doesn't matter who's in front of him. He has to go that way, despite the consequences. Because behind him is the wall, and no option to move.

I also shared a saying with the youth in the gym that day. I learned it from somewhere in the grapevine: "You can't control your fate, but you can control your fight." The chaotic, unpredictable events of life are out of your control. But your response is within your power. I was controlling my fight when fate dragged me down to my lowest point.

Sometimes, your lowest points in life can give birth to your greatest points in life. Let me run that back: *Your lowest points in life can give birth to your greatest points in life.* That's when you need your greatest self. There's no other option.

> **Your lowest points in life can give birth to your greatest points in life.**

Your bottom is primetime for a bounceback. It's an opportunity. *A moment to rise.* That's what I told the young people. I could feel the speech hitting home, energies shifting in the gym. Some of their parents were there too, eagerly listening to the story.

I remember one young man and neighborhood leader, Alex, messaged me a few weeks after my accident:

"My grandma found out about the accident in the neighborhood, and she was saying it was you who got hit. I couldn't believe it. I didn't wanna believe it. I was mad, sad, angry. I'm here now at the gym helping your mom. Ima make you proud david, rest my boi."

He was a sophomore in high school at the time, and I was laid up on the couch when I read that. I was exhausted from my daily rehab exercises, but after seeing that, I went *back to work*. Seeing my story lighting fires in other neighborhood kids kept mine burning too.

Successful Bouncebacks

While I was stuck on that couch, I devoured articles, videos, and any content I could find on successful bouncebacks. Of course, my biggest inspiration was Vinny Pazienza's bounce back after a broken spine. There were others, though.

Adrian Peterson bounced back within eight months after tearing his ACL and MCL to secure the NFL MVP award and one of the greatest rushing seasons in history. Shaun Livingston suffered a similar leg injury as mine but still bounced back into an NBA champion. Zach LaVine tore his ACL and bounced back into an All-Star, reportedly saying he felt even more explosive. Steve Jobs bounced back after being fired from Apple, only to later take the company back and turn it around. Kevin Durant bounced back from tearing his achilles to dominating the international men's basketball scene in the Olympics. Russell Westbrook bounced back after Durant left him, averaging a triple-double and winning the league MVP. And of course, Kobe Bryant's bounceback in just eight months after tearing his achilles as seen on the MUSE documentary.

I needed examples. Proof of concepts. Something to find inspiration and hope. And I knew I had the opportunity to make my life another great example.

One of my favorite bouncebacks was from a TikTok based on a cartoon.

In *Kung Fu Panda 2*, the main character is a Panda named Po, who hits one of his lowest points. A TikTok video by @aaronuribe21 features a low-point scene from the movie with the song "Living Life in the Night" by Cheriimoya & Sierra Kidd in the background.

Po was beaten down, battered, and bruised by his enemies. Head tilted low, eyes closing in despair. He was on the brink of losing it all. His friend Tigris was hanging on to the edge of a boat. His sensei was laid out on floating wreckage. His enemies had their sights locked in on him with several cannons full of iron fireballs, ready to launch. Everything was at its worst. And in that dark moment of hanging on the edge of life, Po pulls out the greatest move ever.

Po reversed the cannon fire coming from his enemies. He redirected the fireballs and sent them back, hurling them towards the cannons that fired them. Po channeled the firepower of those who wanted to destroy him and used it to his advantage. He bounced back when his people needed it most.

I watched that video on repeat hundreds of times.[32] Pulling yourself up from the edge of a cliff is sometimes where the answer hides itself. *The brink of failure can be the brink of greatness.*

Bouncebacks are a beautiful thing. They test you, see what you're made of. You should see them as an opportunity—a fun challenge, a chance to prove how much you've got in the tank. Some of my lowest points in life have led to breakthroughs in dream-chasing. Those moments are the building blocks of your character.

Take the loss of my Dad—I was lost and frustrated with the world, yet I harnessed those emotions to honor my dad through the greatest academic performance of my life. Take the pandemic—I was stuck in my room, isolated, but I used that solitude to do all the research and legwork needed to launch a nonprofit. Or a breakup—I was stuck in my head, devastated, but I redirected that energy into writing this book you have in your hands here today.

I'm not saying ignore your emotions or deny your healing process. I am saying let your emotions flow as they please. And *find ways to capitalize on moments of fragility and chaos*.

> **Find ways to capitalize on moments of fragility and chaos.**

Shortly after graduating from college, I gave a speech at Cabrillo and Wilson High Schools to groups of young men in the Elevate Your Game program—one I was in myself. I talked about how you can't control the things that happen in life, but you are in charge of your response. It had the same sentiment as the speech I gave to Books & Buckets youth five years later.

You can take responsibility for your next move. Don't get caught up in the blaming game. Don't play the victim for too long. When you hit rock bottom, it takes everything you've got to climb out.

I'm not here to just brag about comebacks. I'm here to help you navigate your bottoms. For anyone in need of a bounce-back, I'd recommend the following:

1. **Motivation**: Find Your Fuel
    - Find what inspires you. What lights a fire in you. Create a mental vision of it and replay it in your

head over and over again. Make it a recurring movie in your mind. Use videos, quotes, or stories to help keep the fire burning. Surround yourself with reminders. Change your phone's wallpaper. Put something on the fridge and bathroom mirror, anything to keep it front and center.

2. **Knowledge**: Measure & Research

   - Measure: You want to do this with an intricate understanding of your situation. Measure the obstacle from every angle. How deep is your hole? Use hard data for precision, but also gather stories that help you grasp the severity of it. Identify how to accurately measure progress. This will gauge whether you're headed in the right direction or not.

   - Research: Devour everything related to the challenge in front of you. Watch any informational videos that make you wiser about the problem you are trying to solve. Speak with someone who has successfully navigated a similar situation. But most of all, *read*. Books are the most powerful tool in a bounceback. You retain the information better and get into the granular details.

3. **Protocol**: Create the System

   - Write down your plays and what you're seeking. This helps you stay organized throughout the long journey ahead. Define your sole objective. Break it down into campaigns. Map out the specific and precise actions needed to make it happen.

   - *Objective*: Select a sole objective, goal, target, or north star. I prefer focusing on only one, so it can get everything I got. It also makes decision-making clear. Make sure it's measurable with a set date of completion. Your actions can be driven by one question: Does this get me closer to my objective?

- *Campaigns*: these are the strategies, projects, or operations you take as short-term sprints toward the main objective. The sole objective can be multi-faceted, requiring different angles of direction. Campaigns let you acutely drill in with renewed interest.
- *Tactics*: the specific step-by-step actions needed. Tactics will drive your routine. These details are what get you there. Every hour, every minute, *every second*.
- *Rewards*: choose a motivating award at the end of accomplishing the objective, or even for difficult campaigns. This can help you keep going when the going gets tough.

4. **Execution**: Time to Deliver
   - Like a UPS man. Like a blue-collar worker. Like a factory worker clocking in. Like *Cinderella Man* fighting to keep the fridge full. Like a mom keeping her kids safe. Like a house cleaner with bills to pay. This is the follow-through. That final lap in the mile run that takes everything you got. You have to get this right; otherwise, you don't stand a chance. Be true to your word. Stick to the plan. Put in the work. Don't let your mind trick you. It's okay to adjust the plan as things evolve, as long as those changes support your evolution. Don't make changes that set you back.

5. **Mentality**: Embrace the Pain
   - Bouncebacks are so much sweeter the harder the journey is. The larger the dragon, the greater the tale. Embrace the suffering as part of the process. See it as beneficial suffering. Pain can be a test of greatness. Life isn't Lucky Charms all the time. Sometimes we gotta keep our heads down and get it in. Don't be afraid to suffer a bit. Purposeful suffering makes a conquest feel great. Suffering makes it a resilient, beautiful story.

You got this.

Challenges in life can make you stronger. Some of the strongest-willed people you will ever meet are those who walked through the deepest, darkest trenches of life. Challenges are opportunities to bring out the best in you.

Battles either fold you or mold you. Let them mold you into someone greater than you were before. Even if you fall off initially, because that happens to the best of us, keep the intent intact. Keep the perspective that you will get back up, one way or another. You don't need to know how long it will take. Or how hard it will be. But you must unequivocally feel that you will rise again.

*"You may write me down in history
With your bitter, twisted lies,
You may trod me in the very dirt
But still, like dust, I'll rise."*

Maya Angelou

(My mom babysitting me while I catch some sunlight with Chelly)

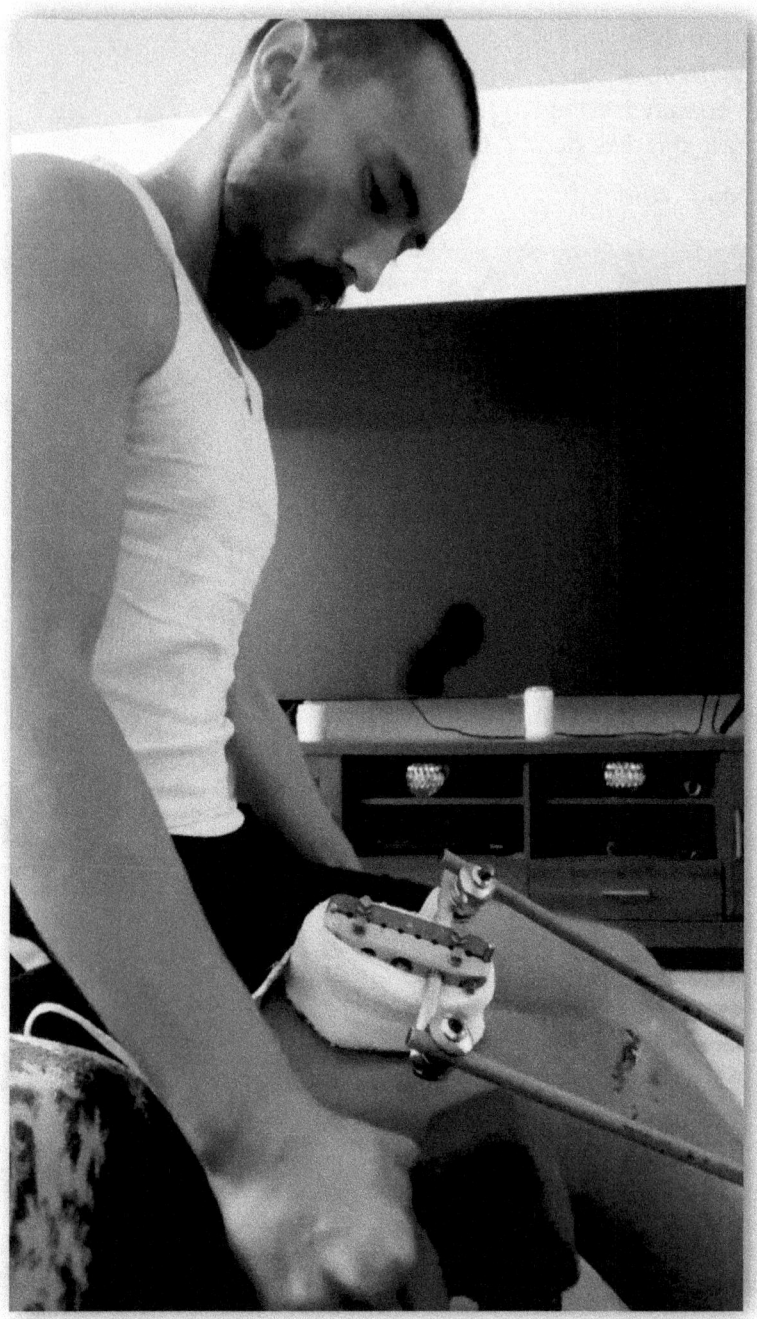
(First ime lifting weights with my external fixator)

(Screenshot from a video of my speech that Media Director Andy Duong posted on Books & Buckets' Instagram)

CHAPTER 9
WHAT IT MEANS TO MAKE IT OUT

Getting run over by that car was one of the best things that has ever happened to me.

I could've died. Remember how I thought the neighborhood would take me out one day? The collision shook me up, reminding me how precious this life is. A second chance. One I will never take for granted. The whole recovery process made me realize that I don't have to annihilate myself in the process of saving my neighborhood. I don't have to be a martyr for the movement.

You don't have to succumb to the ongoing neighborhood plight in the process of making it better. These problems weren't created overnight. You can make your neighborhood better while making yourself better at the same time.

Get Better

Conquering your internal battles is similar to making your neighborhood better, rather than just making it out.

When we're faced with trauma, fear, stressors, conflict, anxiety, or heartache, we often want to make it out of those feelings. We turn to external stimuli like alcohol, smoking, degrading drugs, porn, reckless casual sex, junk food, excessive social media, inundating binge-watching—anything to get us out of our heads. That's *making it out* of your mind. That's not *making it better*.

See, it's in tune with the neighborhood wavelength. Confronting your own struggles instead of just escaping them is similar to confronting your neighborhood's struggles instead of just checking out. You should make it better in your head by focusing on your soul, releasing your emotions, training your mind, confronting and transcending trauma, practicing awareness, sleeping well, putting down social media, working out, elevating (not degrading) plants and supplements, eating whole foods, walking in nature, and fostering meaningful, loving relationships. Those traits can help you make it better, not just make it out. Bring that same energy to the neighborhood.

Don't use your weekends to only run from life's stressors. Use your weekends to also create the life you want to live. The same goes for your community. Don't just make it out and never come back. Make it better. Lift up your neighborhood in all aspects, just as you lift yourself up.

Make it Out

The dream Izzy and I had about "making it out" by any means necessary wasn't unique. Many youth who grow up in disinvested neighborhoods share that same dream. Actors, musicians, and athletes often preach about their tough upbringing and how they reached stardom, often crediting a drive to escape their stress-filled environment.

The concept of "making it out" is discussed in Trevor Noah's book, *Born A Crime*. Noah states that American youth focus on making it out of the hood, which is different from South African youth, where leaving the hood isn't an option. Instead, South African youth are forced to transform the hood. This idea of transformation puts responsibility on residents to not just take flight but to become creators of their environment. American youth have more opportunities to escape their surroundings, which lets go of any responsibility to transform it. It's like staying in a hotel. You know you are about to leave, so it's easier to leave the place all messy. It won't be your problem once you check out.

Well, you can't check out of the neighborhood that raised you. Yeah, you can leave and go explore. You should experience other places this vast, prolific world has to offer. And at the same time, it should always be a collective responsibility to make your neighborhood better, regardless of whether you're still living there or not. No housekeeping is coming to clean up your childhood room.

Transforming the neighborhood means making it a place where people love living in, where there's pride over one's community and a sense of duty to protect it. A nonprofit in Chicago, *My Block, My Hood, My City*, eloquently embodies this vision.[33] Founder Jahmal Cole understands what it takes to shift conditions holding problems in place. He emphasizes that even when massive social issues feel too overwhelming, you can still change yourself and do something simple for your neighborhood.

One of their programs highlights young people telling the story of their neighborhoods through pride, resilience, and awareness over where they come from. Employing youth-led walking tours in South Side Chicago, young people showcase the strengths, gems, and areas of growth in the place they call home. This storytelling practice challenges the notorious narratives of the South Side, reshaping how the next generation of leaders sees the place that raised them.

Another model place-based initiative is the Harlem Children's Zone, led by Geoffrey Canada. In *Whatever It Takes* by Paul Tough, Canada's journey to transform a twenty-four-block zone of Central Harlem is chronicled. Canada wanted Harlem youth to stay where they were with the hopes of changing the entire neighborhood and the neighborhood changing them in the process. He implemented a cradle-to-career approach that emphasized a college-bound strategy. Canada felt that if more Harlem youth graduated from college, they would, in turn, influence those around them to do the same. He didn't want his youth to beat the odds. He wanted them to change the odds. The focus was on population-level change, where impacting one group of kids would have a contagious impact on all the kids in the neighborhood. He brought science to the outcomes, with hopes of real results, not just "feel-good" work. The zone had about 3,000 children, comparable to the Washington Neighborhood.

At Books & Buckets, we employed a similar approach of always thinking about the larger neighborhood at hand. That's why our youth focused on transforming the infrastructure around them. We may only have 20 youth in the gym, but the work they embark on will have a positive impact on the health and safety of the several thousand young people who live in the neighborhood. Books & Buckets may not directly serve several thousand youth at one time, but the levers shifted in creating a more robust neighborhood will reap benefits to every family in the area. If the youth secure a community center, every young person in the neighborhood will benefit from that, even if they never walk into the building. The community center can make the overall neighborhood safer.

A group of youth can go on to live the most successful lives in history, but what does that mean for the neighborhood? For the ones who never even enrolled in our program? We wanted their quality of life in the neighborhood to increase as we lifted others in tandem. We focused on overarching issues that would benefit every young person in the neighborhood, regardless of whether we never worked with them.

Passive Impact Projects

It only takes a generation to decide that just making it out of the hood is not going to cut it. We need to make the neighborhood a place you don't want to make it out of because of how much joy and love it brings you. The hood's challenges will persist if those who succeed leave without a plan to return and reinvest. That's a brain drain. So many talented people come from tough neighborhoods and go on to build lucrative lives, yet their hometowns remain violent, under-resourced, and neglected.

I know this process takes time. Submitting yourself to the daily stressors of the hood when you have the chance to leave for a more supportive environment doesn't make logistical sense. I'm not asking anyone to live under toxic circumstances. I moved out of the neighborhood about a year after my accident because I couldn't stand having a window view of the crosswalk where I was run over. I may even leave Long Beach to explore other neighborhoods around the world. Who knows? But what I am asking is that we stay connected to the neighborhood in some meaningful way.

I'm not talking about once-a-year backpack giveaways, Christmas toy drives, or one-off community cleanups just for a feel-good photo op. No more just superficial handouts. What we need is intentionality and mutual cycle-breaking. I'm talking about sustainable backbone organizations, innovative initiatives, transformative businesses, significant financial investments, mobilization efforts at city hall, and relentlessly feeling responsible for making it better.

Create sustainable projects that scale over time, regardless of how involved you are. *Plant seeds—scalable community projects that continue to grow like a flower through the concrete of distress.* These are *passive impact projects*. The impact of the neighborhood passively increases over time, with or without you. They morph, transform, evolve. Their work advances toward sustainable change that lasts for generations. Because it might take generations.

Plant seeds—scalable community projects that continue to grow like a flower through the concrete of distress

My nonprofit is a passive impact project. A seed I planted that will keep growing in the garden of the neighborhood until it is no longer needed to bear fruit. I no longer lead day-to-day decision-making for Books & Buckets. It scales at its own pace with its autonomous leadership. Its impact will always be felt.

The 14th Street Park Revitalization project is a seed *también*. The transformation of the courts will always play a role in the development of neighborhood youth. Bringing a community center to the neighborhood is another passive impact project. Once the center gets built, neighborhood kids will use that facility for generations. Even this book is a seed. The message of *making your neighborhood better* will inspire the next generation of neighborhood kids to take back their communities from the tyranny of violence and social disorganization. The message is being passed on for the work to continue, no matter what I do as I round out my late 20s. Environmental levers were shifted in their grooves, building a snowball momentum of neighborhood liberation.

The best way to escape the issues in our neighborhoods isn't by running away and retreating. It's by facing them head-on until they are solved. Change the environment around you. Make it better. That's the best way to make it out of the stressors of gang violence, poverty, housing insecurity, and neglect. If you can change those issues, you genuinely *made it out of them*.

Coffee Bean

Author Damon West shares a story he learned in prison from a fellow inmate named Mr. Jackson. He compares prison to a pot of hot water, where your initiation can go one of three ways. When you drop a carrot in hot water, it gets soft and weak, damaged by external stressors. When you drop an egg in hot water, it hardens, less open for life, and more rugged. When you drop a coffee bean in hot water, the water becomes coffee. It's no longer called water. Mr. Jackson advised West to not be an egg or a carrot in prison, but instead to become a coffee bean. The coffee bean changes its surroundings.

That's the energy our neighborhoods need. Being a coffee bean means taking the heat, the challenges of the hood, and using it to transform your environment. It's a call to create something better, not letting the battles tell you who to be. Change how the neighborhood is built rather than letting it change you. Be a coffee bean for the neighborhood.

$$\text{Environment} \rightarrow \text{makes you} \rightarrow \text{soft}$$
$$\text{Environment} \rightarrow \text{makes you} \rightarrow \text{hard}$$
$$\text{Environment} \leftarrow \text{your} \leftarrow \text{you make}$$

Act Local

Future NBA Hall of Famer DeMar DeRozan is the epitome of loyal to the local. Growing up in Compton, DeRozan was a standout athlete. High schools all over the country were recruiting him, including Oak Hill, which was a private school known for turning out NBA stars like Carmelo Anthony and Kevin Durant. DeRozan turned Oak Hill down and decided to make his hometown, Compton High School, into a powerhouse team. Compton wasn't known for basketball prior to DeRozan. He turned them into a monster program and brought them a league title. DeRozan chose to build up the legacy of his local surroundings, rather than just adding his talent to an established elite.

DeRozan came out to my last high school basketball game against Compton because they were retiring his jersey that night. We got obliterated. But it was so cool to see him at a Cabrillo High versus Compton High game. I remember knocking down a three and staring at him to see if he saw it. That jersey would have never gone up the rafters if he went to Oak Hill or some other dominant private school. He created a legacy for the school and recognition for other athletes to go there for the years following. He is known for always coming back to the block that raised him.

Too often, when people make it big in their craft, they get caught up in the broader landscape of giving back and lose track of the local. Local is the block you grew up on. Your neighborhood park and school. Local is the stomping grounds where you rode your bike on. Focusing on the local doesn't always look the coolest because there might not be a nationwide movement or media presence behind it. But local is where you can actually get something done.

Many of the issues we see on the international and national stages are ones we have little impact on. With that said, one thing you can always do is step outside your front door and have a direct impact on your local community.

Our energy and attention should be devoted to things within our influence. You should act local. It's something you have a direct, measurable effect on.

Invest in the tranquility of your block.

Invest in the camaraderie of your community.

Invest in the relationships that make you feel like you belong.

Don't worry so much about who dropped a new diss track. *Worry about the diss tracks your neighborhood's been hit with—violence, isolation, neglect.*

See through the noise. Act local.

Don't "Just" Make It Out

This book is about a neighborhood kid who wanted to make it out of his neighborhood. Then he realized he could make it better, too. And he could make himself better in the process. That his neighborhood didn't have to make him worse. That he didn't have to make himself worse to make his neighborhood better. He could make them both better.

The concept "don't just make it out, make it better" brands the idea that making it out is not separate from making it better. Meaning, you don't have to choose between one or the other. They aren't binary. Making it better is actually a form of making it out.

In the word smithing of "don't just make it out, make it better," I don't cancel the "make it out" part. I added the "just" right before it because I completely understand when it's time for you to leave. A childhood friend of mine left the neighborhood after being targeted by the local gang. His life was in danger, so he had to let it go. But he hasn't forgotten about the neighborhood. He's still connected.

That's why there is a "just" in the phrase "don't just make it out, make it better." There's power in exploring the world, living in other communities, and experiencing other cultures. But you can't *just* leave without being a part of the long game.

Revitalizing a local basketball court is something achievable. Creating a community mural is a long-lasting endeavor. Bringing a community center to the area can be done in partnership with local leaders. Buying out problematic apartments and converting them into affordable home-ownership opportunities reshapes the neighborhood's infrastructure. Replacing liquor stores with grocery stores and transforming food banks into mutual aid farmers' markets changes the quality of nutrition, bringing agency in the process. Providing transition homes, mom-and-pop businesses, sports complexes, creative hubs, and wrap-around holistic healing centers focuses more on turning off the faucet of problems rather than *just* mopping up the water that was spilled.

Local change can lead to cascades of regional transformation. Just because it's local, doesn't mean there's no impact regionally. One neighborhood at a time.

Don't just aim to leave. Transform. Build. Reinvest.

The legacy of your neighborhood depends on it.

CHAPTER 10
HOW TO CHANGE THE NEIGHBORHOOD

In 2023, during the Q&A section of the gang prevention panel, a young woman spoke up:

"Where do I start? Like, I love everything that was discussed here, but I want to know how I can prevent violence in the neighborhood. How can I help you all?"

It was a genuine, well-meaning question. People want to contribute.

One of our panelists, Miguel Lugo from Homeboy Industries, encouraged her to join a local organization and volunteer her time. Other panelists chimed in with similar recommendations, emphasizing the importance of donating to organizations doing the work.

People just need a formula sometimes. They want the protocol. Instructions manual. Playbook. Roadmap. It's not fair to expect people to work on their cars without providing them with an owner's manual. It's kind of crazy how we don't provide an owner's manual for ourselves, for our neighborhoods. This chapter serves as the owner's manual for transforming your neighborhood and yourself.

Systems Change

I was first introduced to the concept of systems change while working for The Nonprofit Partnership. My supervisor, Christina, gave me this report to read: *The Water of Systems Change* by John Kania, Mark Kramer, and Peter Senge from FSG Reimagining Social Change.[34] It outlines the different levers that should be addressed to create sustainable, long-term change that shifts conditions holding long-standing problems in place.

The report highlights how we often work on social issues without actually solving them. We feed into a system that lives off a problem rather than an endpoint solution. This framework is designed to bring real endpoint solutions. Here's a remixed, neighborhood breakdown of the levers:

- **Power Dynamics**
    - Who holds decision-making power in your neighborhood? Where does hard power live? This can be neighborhood association presidents, City Councilmembers, the Mayor, the police Chief, block captains, park supervisors, school principals, philanthropists, state legislators, Congressmembers, directors of community-based organizations, business owners, pastors and priests—anyone who has a significant impact on your community's quality of life. The focus is on engaging these power holders in addressing the problems of the neighborhood and investing in the solutions that need their support.
- **Policies**
    - These are the rules that govern where you live. Policymakers write them, and they can either clean up some of the mess in the neighborhood or make it messier. Think about which rules cause more harm than good, and which rules are needed to organize the way of life. Push local leaders to support policies

that will benefit the neighborhood. It's hard to make headway on this one without experts in policy. It's a complex topic. On a smaller scale, you can change some of the local rules. For example, street sweeping times in the Washington Neighborhood are from 5 am to 8 am. Yet, across town in the wealthier areas, the times are often 10 am to 12 pm or 12 pm to 2 pm. I grew up hearing my neighbors move their cars around 4:30 am, then sleep in them until the sweeper passed just to secure their spot. It's not fair that the neighborhood with the highest levels of stress also forces its residents to move their cars before dawn to avoid a $75 ticket, while other areas don't even worry about it because the times fall during regular working hours. You can change this rule.

- **Practices**
  - Practices shape customs, structure, traditions, and mannerisms of a community. For example, a monthly neighborhood meal is a prosocial practice that brings the community together to break bread and connect. On the other hand, proving your manhood by harming other young men is a destructive practice in criminal street gang culture. Evaluate practices in your community. Think about the ones you should give more life to or let go of.

- **Community Power**
  - How united is your community? If you need to pull up to an important meeting with some comrades to show strength in the cause, how many of your neighbors would stand with you? When there's strong community power, communication is smooth, leading to a quick and collective response when something goes down. This fuels mobilization efforts. Rally your neighbors around something everyone can agree on. Host consistent community

meetings to keep relationships intact. Your practices can support the formation of community power: regular neighborhood meals or community mixers. Being around each other can build trust and camaraderie. Once that bond is there, folks will have each other's backs when it's time to take a stand.

- **Resources**
  - All lasting change requires funding. Understanding power dynamics helps you leverage resources from those in power. But resources go beyond money. Community-based organizations can provide volunteers. City departments can lend items needed for a clean-up. Still, money is the most critical resource because it lets you freely source what you need. Secure funding through crowdfunding, grants, sponsorships, elected officials, or wealthy individuals. If you can figure out how to bring in dollars, the rest will fall into place.
- **Beliefs**
  - This may be the toughest one. Mental models refer to the ideologies and beliefs that people hold. Earlier, I shared how a park supervisor believed gang violence has always been around and always will be. That belief rejects hope for a better tomorrow, free of gang violence. You want to support an ecosystem where the neighborhood's beliefs contribute to a thriving community. Consider the beliefs that may need some upgrades. Think about new, uplifting ideas you want to introduce in your community.

Systems change takes work, and all these levers can feel daunting and overwhelming. For anyone looking to take the first steps in helping their neighborhood/vecindario evolve, the foundation is developing a healthy sense of ownership and pride over it. *Build out that identity.* That's what ignites the fire to take action and protect it.

Participating in something can develop identity. When you participate in a local clean-up, you feel more connected to your surroundings. You take ownership over them. When you help paint a community mural, you remember the brush strokes that led to that masterpiece. And you look out for it when someone tags it up because you remember the time, sweat, and energy you sacrificed for it. You worked for it.

The identity also comes from storytelling. Every time you share core memories about your neighborhood, it reminds you how much it means to you. Just like the Chicago youth who led the walking tours. They paint their own picture of the place they grew up in. Honoring your local parks, schools, and libraries with love and pride creates the responsibility to take care of it. It's another reminder that it's theirs. In the ups and downs of it all. Their neighborhood. Their identity.

Once that pride is internalized, follow these **4Ys**:

Your Block

The corner-to-corner stretch you live on or grew up on. It's what you walk by every time you head to school or work. It's the last thing you see before calling it a night. You should be a Block Captain: someone who looks out for the health and safety of their block. That can mean helping your neighbor take out the trash, bringing in the groceries, or clearing the alley of all those beds and cabinets. A great Block Captain knows their neighbors and develops meaningful relationships. It's the simple things here that count.

Your Neighborhood

This is the close-knit community you live in, usually bordered by four main streets. Once you get the block down, you're ready to be a neighborhood leader: someone who takes charge of local issues and speaks up for the needs of the area. Neighborhood leaders bring the community together through communal events and places of camaraderie. Most neighborhoods have a park, a school, and some businesses. Use them as places of refuge. Organize an event in your community. Be creative. It can be a clean-up, a walk audit, a watch party, or a neighborhood meal. Make sure to attend your neighborhood association meetings if you have one. If you don't, consider starting one. You can even create one to unite young people. You can call it Neighborhood Kids, depending on the name of your neighborhood. Neighborhood associations are often dominated by individuals who are negative, grumpy, and frustrated. Starting with new, naive energy will open up the door to innovative solutions. As you organize, try not to get caught up in personality clashes or ego trips. I say that because neighborhood leaders can become power-hungry and make it about themselves. Stay humble, and if you feel that energy from a neighborhood leader, be mindful not to feed into it, but don't cut them off either. If you do, then you'll be a part of the problem. Stand strong as united neighborhood leaders, with the mindset of making your community one of the best in the city.

Your City

A great deal of what goes on in your neighborhood is shaped by the decisions made at the city government level. Local politicians, such as Councilmembers and the Mayor, directly impact the neighborhood. Attend City Council meetings and see what's up. Attend City events. Meet your elected officials. Shake their hands. Talk about your neighborhood. See if you can collaborate on a project. Consider serving on a City Commission, Committee, Coalition, Council, task force, or whatever they call their leadership bodies. Share your voice at City Hall on topics that you care about. Get involved. Maybe even run for office if you feel the traction. You should know your city well. *Your city should know you.*

Yourself

How can you serve the community when you haven't even served yourself? This is the most important one. I need you to wake up and let it sink in. It took a serious accident for me to fully comprehend this. It's easy to neglect yourself when you're so deeply caught up in the mission. But none of that work will be sustainable if you aren't showing yourself the love it deserves. I've seen too many community members working to heal external wounds while carrying internal ones they refuse to acknowledge.

How can you serve the community when you haven't even served yourself?

I've created a roadmap to help navigate the areas of life. I call it THE PLAYBOOK: A guide to life because no one gave me one growing up. Think of it as your life's *starting five*. Use the blank pages in the back of the book to map these areas out now.

THE PLAYBOOK

1. **Spiritual**

- Everyone's spiritual self looks different. Just think about your soul. What feels greater than yourself? It could be a divine power, religion, the universe, nature, a drive to do something meaningful, exploring the world, future existence, or your inner child. Define what it means to you. Reflect on your current state. Think about things you can do to invest in your spiritual self. Read a book on it. Do some experiments. Make some promises to yourself. Take your time here.

2. **Mental**

- Your mind. Your thinking patterns. Your thoughts. This is your conscious self—the voices in your head, the ideas on your mind. You have to be friends with your mind. The biggest one here, from my experience, is *awareness*. I've learned this from trial and error—and from Dr. Joe Dispenza's book, *Becoming Supernatural*. Become hyper-aware of the thoughts that try to enter your mind. Don't let the ones that damage you slip past your awareness. Sometimes, you're so lost in the sauce that you aren't even *aware* you are going through something in the first place. Just become aware of what your mind sways to and use positive practices to help steer it in the right direction. Some common practices include meditation, gratitude practice, presence, cultivating elevated emotions, mantras, visualizations, or neurocycling.

3. **Emotional**

- Ever hear someone say, "I feel like a weight has been lifted off my shoulders"? It's because they were releasing emotions that were weighing them down. Once they were able to say what they needed to say, the emotion flowed out of them rather than staying blocked and repressed. I was in one relationship when I was younger, where I felt a constant tight feeling in my stomach. It was a ball of anxiety. I tried punching bags, screaming my lungs out during every Laker game, and anything I could think of at the time. It helped, but it didn't truly get released until I told the person I was with that it was probably best that we weren't together. It was something deep down I felt because of how different we were. I didn't want to say it because I loved her so much and didn't want to lose her. I remember crying uncontrollably after I said it. But I felt open again. The tightness disappeared.
- Your emotions can take a toll on your body if you aren't releasing them. Let them flow. Cry when you need to cry. Get angry when you can safely get angry.

Use practices to help release these emotions. There are psychosomatic exercises for anger or sadness release, such as Ashley Velvet Frost's anger exercises on YouTube or Dr. Christian Gonzalez's 5-day emotional alchemy newsletter.

- Sports and music create space for emotional expression. Screaming at the top of your lungs after a big play in a game helps release the anger you have about what someone said to you at work. Singing and crying to a song that hits deep can help release the sadness you were hiding. Singing, crying, dancing, laughing, humming, screaming, punching, jumping, running, lifting, flexing, and telling people how you really feel are modes of expression that create momentum to release repressed emotions.

4. **Physical**
- Your actual body that takes up space. Your surrounding infrastructure. Your skin, hair, heart, brain, or gut. It involves all your organs. The vessel you inhabit. You only get one. Take care of it. There is so much information out there. Sleep is your foundation. Movement should be a daily habit. Eating wholesome foods will make your organs thank you. Conduct quantitative measurements if you can: blood panels, organic acid tests, GI maps, wearables, continuous glucose monitors, MRIs, etc. Take care of that beautiful body, baby.

5. **Social**

- I once dated someone who felt they didn't hang out at bars that much. I felt the contrary. She was at bars multiple times a week, every weekend, and during weekdays. All the bouncers knew her. She felt it wasn't that much because she was comparing it to her friends who were bartenders, DJs, and people who spent their free time having a drink and a smoke at a local dive bar. I compared it to my friends, who usually spent their weekends attending sporting events, finishing up their graduate studies, camping, or rising early to catch the sunrise. I'm not here to be the moral judge and say which is better. I am nobody; make your own conclusions. But I can objectively conclude that they were just too different. Our relative base measurements were not aligned. It obviously didn't work out, despite how much I was into her.

- The behaviors you engage in are very similar to your social circles. That circle unintentionally serves as a relative measure of how your life is going. There's a Mexican saying that goes, "Dime con quién andas, y yo te diré quién eres." Tell me who you are around, and I'll tell you who you are. Our social circles dictate how we live and view our own lives. Choose wisely.

- Your social component involves friends, family, a significant other, identity, work, finances, hobbies, socioeconomic status, and anything else in the *games* you play with fellow humans in this world. I include work here because a majority of your time will be spent around your coworkers, not your friends. They influence you and are part of your social life. People like to think they are separate, but they aren't. The social interactions we experience at work are just as significant as the ones we have outside of it. We are not robots. We must find joy in the ones we clock in with and be mindful of how they are influencing us.

All areas of life are interconnected. You can focus most of your energy on one, but that doesn't mean you neglect the rest. I like to do these in order, starting with the Spiritual and then making my way down, referencing an expert in each field. The most important project you will ever work on is yourself. Project YOU. You are the CEO of YOU. Take responsibility for it. How can you support the neighborhood when you can't even support yourself? *Get to work.* Make an action plan. Implement a revitalization plan in your own life before you do it for the community.

Your block. Your neighborhood. Your city. *Yourself.* It starts with what's *yours.*

Now, I haven't fully figured it out myself, so add your own twist to it. These frameworks are just stepping stones to help us get there.

When I think of all the areas that need work in the neighborhood, I am left with about four pillars: housing, healing, working, and educating. When I first thought about this, I was walking around Seaside Park asking myself, "What would it take?" What would it take to really change things around, because our youth programs are just a drop of water in a dry desert. It needs a wrap-around view. If resources were plentiful, these would be the areas I would prioritize:

- **Housing**: Buy up all the run-down, problematic apartments in the neighborhood. Generously compensate families to pursue affordable home ownership options. Turn all the land into single-family homes or affordable condos, ensuring those who grew up here—and bring love here—have the opportunity to buy in.
- **Healing**: Allocate substantial funds to hire therapists, somatic practitioners, peacekeepers, psychologists, medical doctors, and holistic wellness professionals to heal the hood from the traumas of the past. *Confront those skeletons in the closet so the community can break free from the shackles of violence.*

- **Working**: Create financial incentives that allow people to work in careers they love and excel at. Leverage funding as a tool for outreach and engagement in sought-after fields. Hire community outreach workers to help strengthen collective efficacy in the neighborhood. Help people find meaning and purpose in their craft.
- **Educating**: Pay for people to finish their high school education, undergraduate studies, graduate studies, and doctorates. Offer a myriad of youth education programs across the six domains (sports, music, art, STEM, entrepreneurship, and civics). Turn the area into an educated hub of neighborhood leaders. Cultivate a culture of lifelong learning.

Everything revolves around *ideas and decisions*. You get an idea to do something, and you decide to do it or not. It's that simple. People try to make it seem more complex, but it's not. All these different frameworks are just ideas. And ideas are great, but they don't have any impact until you make that *decision*. The decision to act. The decision to step up. That's what turns ideas into tangible results for a community.

Everyone has ideas. But not everyone makes an unwavering decision to make things happen.

It's time for you to decide. Who are you?

(The crosswalk on Pacific & 16th)

(Youth leader Mario grabbing his new book—2022)

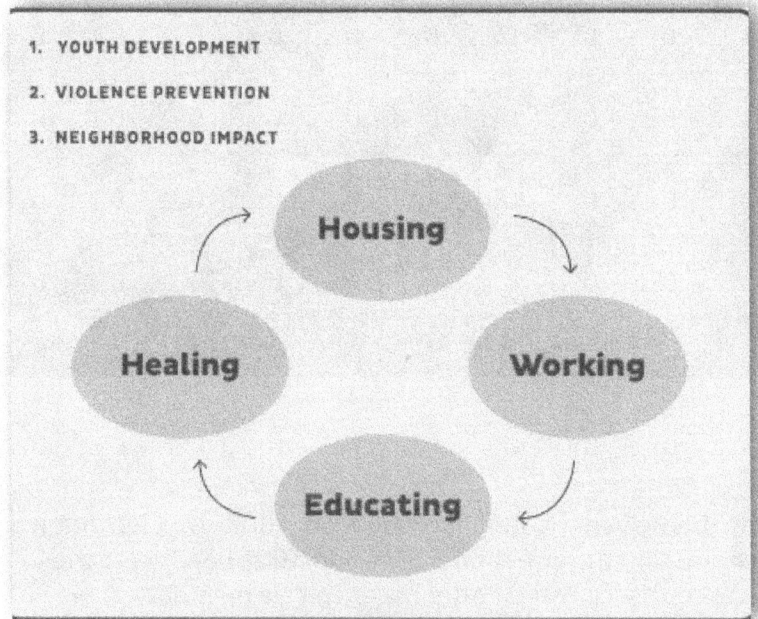

(Graph from Books & Buckets Strategic Plan designed by City Fabrick)

CHAPTER ∞
CONCLUSION: JUST A NEIGHBORHOOD KID

I'll always be a neighborhood kid. I'll always be that kid crossing the street off Pacific and 16th, heading to the local courts. Doesn't matter my age. It's a mentality. A way of understanding how my inner child aligns with the upbringing of my neighborhood. How I was shaped and crafted. *Brick by brick, that neighborhood built me.*

I want people to remember where they come from. So much so, they feel the need to protect it and help it evolve. A neighborhood kid never forgets the community that raised her. A neighborhood kid stands tall in the face of social problems. A neighborhood kid solves the violence and disorganization within themselves before trying to solve it for a community.

Everyone has that neighborhood kid inside them. It's just about listening, giving that neighborhood kid a voice.

Anyone can be a neighborhood kid. My neighborhood kid story started when my mom immigrated to the United States in search of a new life. She crossed the border several times, got caught repeatedly, and kept going. She did it while pregnant, running and jumping through rough terrain, and even straight through checkpoints. Growing up with an undocumented mom meant never knowing if she'd still be home or snatched up by immigration enforcement. Her journey to this country led to this neighborhood kid. Without her, there'd be no nonprofit, no book, no programs, no offices, no campaigns, and no projects. Undocumented families anchor many of our *barrios*, cultivating some of the hardest-working morale you have ever seen. A neighborhood kid can be built from any humble beginning.

When someone picks up this book, the neighborhood kid inside of them should get fired up, ready to face life's obstacles head-on. *Face the flames*. I want them to gain something practical, not just bluff, hoo-rah-rah, and "look at me." I want them to use the combination of storytelling and frameworks to become creators in their own lives, not just consumers.

People, Places, & Books

The three modalities that have resulted in the most wisdom and growth in my life are the people I've met, the places I've been, and, of course, the books I've read.

The humans who enter your life are either elevating or degrading your quality of experience. Some add wisdom through their lived experience. Others influence you to engage in self-sabotage. Meeting people who bring value to your life can have a dramatic impact on how you experience this game—how you play it. They can help you navigate challenges, champion obstacles, and channel lessons from your journey. Meet more people who elevate your life. Thought experiment: Imagine if you hung out with the 10 most inspirational people you can think of for an entire year. Who would you become?

Places add to my understanding of how life works. From studying nature to admiring the mesmerizing beauty of architecture to immersing myself in unfamiliar communities, all of it adds data to the memory card of life. The more places you've been, the more of life's secret recipe you'll have written down. Seeing the safaris of Africa brought me a new perspective on humanity. Visiting waterfalls in the Amazon rainforest made me rejoice in the beauty of this world. Visit more places.

The books I have read have had the most powerful impact on my life. You can download someone's 50 years of living wisdom in just one month. You can choose which mistakes and lessons are relevant to your repertoire. We only get one life. *If we limit our knowledge solely to our own experiences, we'll be shortchanged.* Live many lives. Learn from the written life of a great musician, actor, politician, monk, and anyone whom you may not meet in the real world. I might never meet Barack Obama. But when I read his book *A Promised Land*, it felt like I was having a beer with him. His stories became plays I could run or cancel out in my life's playbook.

> **If we limit our knowledge solely to our own experiences, we'll be shortchanged.**

It was my turn to write something that could change the world. This book serves as a sword in battle for our neighborhoods. A tool to carry. A message to embody. Keep finding opportunities to get better. Refuse to get worse.

Neighborhood Attention

We get so caught up in the dramas on the news or the feed that we forget to invest our energy in something that actually makes an impact. People get lost in what this president said about that. Which celebrity has beef with whom. Who broke up with whom. Or how many points they scored on them.

> **We get so caught up in the dramas on the news or the feed that we forget to invest our energy into something that actually makes an impact.**

It's time to take back our *attention* and focus on what truly matters—ourselves, our blocks, our communities. Focus on our own stats rather than the stats of others. Focus on our own conflicts that need resolving, rather than the dramas of people who don't even know you.

I didn't write this book because I've lived the hardest life ever—far from it. Not because I've accomplished the most—far from that too. I wrote it to draw parallels to the problems facing my neighborhood. My stories intertwine with tangible frameworks for addressing issues, developing campaigns, shifting paradigms, and *looking inward*.

Izzy and I don't really talk much anymore. I occasionally run into him in the neighborhood. We catch up, talk about girls, jobs, problems, who just had a baby, who got shot, who got locked up, or just roast each other like old times. We pick up right where we left off.

I don't want the culture of the neighborhood to change. I want the violence and decimation to change. People don't have to be shot, run over, or locked up. Raising awareness about the hardships of a community is a key lever for mobilizing momentum. If no one's paying attention to the tragedies in the neighborhood, there's no pressure to put an end to them. *Our neighborhoods need attention.*

Our neighborhoods need attention.

In 2021, I lost someone I grew up with in the neighborhood. I was reading local news when I saw there was a shooting a block away from me on Pacific and 15th. A man was gunned down while riding his bike. I read the name in the article and froze. I knew him.

Oscar Muñoz Sánchez. I grew up playing basketball with him at the 14th Street courts. He'd always roll up to the courts in his ankle weights, talking about how he was going to start dunking soon. Friendly *carnal*—one of those dudes everyone got along with.

He was killed while riding home to see his two daughters. I'm not sure why. Maybe it was gang-related. Maybe not. What I do know is that we lost a father, a brother, a friend, a neighbor, and a teammate as a result of senseless violence. His daughters and family will feel the gravity of his death for generations.

After I found out about the shooting, I wanted people to know his story. Too often, when people get murdered, their stories get lost down the drain. So I reached out to some contacts I had with the local press and asked them to do a feature on him and his family. Crystal Niebla from the Long Beach Post picked it up. She lived in the neighborhood before, so she had some skin in the game. She covered who he was and his connections to the community. People got to see him as more than just another victim of gun violence. He had a story.[35]

There are so many deaths that don't get any attention. Our neighborhoods, overall, don't get enough attention.

We should put more attention on our local community, not just celebrity drama. We often know more about famous athletes, artists, musicians, and actors than we do about our own neighborhoods. It's similar to how we treat ourselves. We often know more about trends, beef, and mainstream celebrity culture than we do about our own lives.

A culture shift is needed. Because you have a story to share, too.

After reading this book, I hope that the neighborhood kid, parent, professional, or funder will start paying more attention to our most impacted neighborhoods. Attention can manifest in various forms, including press coverage, grants, community events, community centers, and built-environment improvements. If enough people devote their attention to the biggest problems, those problems will give in. But *we can't give in*. We have to keep going. The "keep going" just has to be smarter, faster, stronger—smoother.

We can't keep doing the same old things, turning the same old gears.

Find that neighborhood kid in you. Find that neighborhood spirit. Find that fire.

Because we can't *just* make it out.

We have to make it better, too.

ACKNOWLEDGMENTS

To my neighborhood—I am so grateful to call the Washington Neighborhood my hometown. It raised me into who I am today.

To my mom—Momma took care of her big three and always did her best. I get my fire from you.

To my sisters—Lisa and Denise have always been mother figures to me, making sure I looked fly and knew how to talk to girls. Denise, you always protected me and gave me a ride to the gym whenever I needed it. Lisa, you always cared for me and made sure I wasn't looking ugly.

To my dad—I wish he could've been here to offer a helping ear and some good ol' peer review. He always peer-reviewed my papers over a plate of food at Souplantation. I hope you enjoyed seeing this one through my eyes, Pops.

Thank you to Judith McGill for saving my dad and to all the McGills who treat me like their own: John, Deby, Scott, Wei, Andrew, Ingrid, Johnny, Derek, Lilia, Ryan, Jasmine, Rory, Jana, Jake.

Thank you to the Sorianos for anchoring my mom and reminding me where I come from: Tio Samuel, Tia Angelina, Tio Checo, Jason, Giselle, Alex, Dany, Christopher, Priscila, Tio Jorge, Tia Lupe, Tio Hector, Alondra, y todos mis tíos y primos que no mencioné.

Thank you to all my friends who helped edit this book: Jared, Janice, Avery, Montserrat, Stephanie, Eli, Julian, Fern,

Amir, Jarrod, and Leonidas. I will always honor the time you took to help make this book better. Y'all are some real ones.

Thank you to Izzy for making my childhood an adventure that's worthy enough to write about.

Thank you to Pacific City Lights for making me want to go outside and play with my friends: Izzy, Vincent, Mike, Roger, T.O., Emmanuel, Samuel, Sandra, Lil' Frank, Big Frank, Eric, and all the other neighborhood kids.

Thank you to Jackie Robinson Academy and all my classmates and teachers for making elementary and middle school something I wish I could relive: Arvon, Luis, Asante, Janna, Noah, Johnny, Barry, Jaylen, Deon, Josue, Lheonna, Nancy, Carmela, Josue, Tatyanna, Grace, Mr. Licano, Coach, Sydney, Rihanna, Raegan, and many others.

Thank you to the President of Lakewood Hoops for believing in me even when others didn't. And to all my teammates I shared the concrete court with: Justin, Professor, Pepe, Tyler, Jack, Jacob, Patrick, Pat, and Isaac.

Thank you to Coach Jay and Coach Way for letting this spiky-haired kid play basketball. And thank you to all of Cabrillo High School for giving me the quientessential high school experience: Daisy, Jr, Alejandro, Sequan, Mike, Garret, Rian, Jacob, Dwayne, Izzy, Jamari, Antonio, Ray, Gary, Malcom, Berry, Tylen, Terrance, Lee, Donovan, Angel, Gabe, RaJohn, Janaye, Ms. Pope, Mr. Fisher, Ms. Gastelum, Ms. Montooth, and many others.

Thank you to Chico State, my dorm roommates, and everyone else for making my college experience full of memories worth telling around a campfire: Steph, Charlie, Johnnie, Greg, Sayers, Kiel, Demian, Eli, Tony, Seabass, Roberto, Beef guy Zac, Tim, Roberto, Justin, T-Mainey, Brooks, Nicte, Dom, Dulce, Elsa.

Thank you to Long Beach State, SHPE, and my study abroad class for giving me lifelong friends: Ever, Aldo, Jose,

Geno, Angel, Ricardo, Kevin, Danny, Trieuvy, Jorge, Kenya, Yasmine, Gerrel, Jarrod, Ed, Jen, Alyssa, Christina, and Sabrina.

Thank you to all the travelers I met backpacking around the world for filling my life full of memories I can reminisce on: Sara, Tamare, Julia, Catherine, Tina, Mike, Dustin, Nicole, Honor, Sophie, Tara, Carlotta, and Liam.

Thank you to Dr. Amir Whitaker for taking me under his wing when no one else would.

Thank you to Jared Milrad for making me believe I can change the world.

Thank you to Erik Miller for showing me what a great leader looks like.

Thank you to Christina Hall for taking a chance on me and teaching me systems change work.

Thank you to Ana Lopez for trusting my obsession for a better city.

Thank you to the City of Long Beach for making our city the best it can be: Rex, Tom, Montserrat, Teresa, Leonidas, Alanah, Erica, Stephanie, Adrian, Teil, Eduardo, Yonique, Perla, Morgan, Jacqui, Adelita, Eli, Utilia, Kandi, Carmen, Reza, Reyna, Julian, Jennifer, Jeremy, Amanda, Alison, Wilma, Becca, Ha, Lucius, Joshua, Lexus, Kristen, Lupe, Maria, Anthony, Celeste, Sherlyn, Joy, Susie, Joy, Christina, Alejandra, Gaby, Harold, April, Tyler, Fern, Larry, Ashleigh, Gladys, Taron, Travis, Marcella, Maricela, Heidi, Morgan, Cathy, Detrick, Christian, Clayton, Jacob, Mary, Suely, and so many others.

Thank you to Teresa Gomez for showing me the ropes and always watching my back. You wrote a beath-taking foreword that brough me to tears. You have been one of the most powerful influences in my life over the past few years. Mi reina.

Thank you to the Books & Buckets team for believing we can change the neighborhood: Andrew, Gabe, Andy, Kelly, Travis, Alex, Edrick, Mario, Andrew, Emiliano, Jason, Danny, Andrea, and Marlene.

Thank you to all my friends and family for understanding the time I needed in solitude to finish this book: Ed, Jason, Ricardo, Jorge, Jose, Aldo, Trieuvy, Mike, Arvon, Alejandro, Gabe, Andrew, Julian, Teresa, Montserrat, Adrian, and so many others.

Thank you to Haroulla for always checking in on me and my book's progress. The writing journey was very lonely, but you made it less so.

Thank you to Grammarly and ChatGPT for helping review my writing for grammar and clarity.

Thank you to Amazon KDP for decentralizing the publishing world and making me an indie author.

Thank you to the books that inspired me the most to write this: *Greenlights* by Mathew McConaughey, *Limitless* by Jim Kwik, *Born a Crime* by Trevor Noah, *Think Again* by Adam Grant, *WILL* by Will Smith, *The Diary of a CEO* by Steven Bartlett, *Breaking the Trap* by Dr. Amir Whitaker, *Outlive* by Dr. Peter Attia, *Shoot Your Shot* by Vernon Brundage Jr., *Always Running* by Luis Rodriguez, *Believe in You* by Jared Milrad, *The High Life* by Dr. Dina Perrone, and *Grit, Grind, and Glory* by Anthony McDuffie Jr.

AFTERWORD

I wrote this book fresh out of a rough breakup. It was a period of true introspection and heartache. I lost someone I once thought would be my partner for life. We grew apart. Still, I'm grateful for everything I learned from her. She added value to my life, and when we realized we were too different, we went our separate ways. That relationship helped me evolve as a human and write this book. It was the perfect time to devote my *attention to reflection*.

I ended up finishing the first draft of this book while backpacking through Africa. Anywhere from writing on a janky bus bouncing along safari dirt roads to leaning against a tree in front of the Okavango Delta, listening to hippos sing in the background. I was getting it in.

There's something about a super-long document that feels daunting, discouraging, and never-ending. The more you work on it, the more you realize how much more work it needs. It sometimes feels like quicksand (tap in). And this is coming from someone who knows how to knock out tasks, get things done, and stay productive. I would find every excuse not to work on the book. I only liked working in huge blocks so I could immerse myself in deep work and flow. The substantive stuff doesn't come out in bursts.

Writing the first draft was the first hill to climb. But editing was the tallest hill to climb. Writing a book is way different than starting a nonprofit. Starting a nonprofit involves building community and getting out there. Writing a book is about how much you're willing to suffer while isolated behind a laptop. I spent about 100 hours writing the first draft. Then another 700 hours of editing. Then another 100 hours for publishing and a final 100 hours for marketing. So all in all, it took about 1,000+ hours of locked-in focus to knock this thing out, but the ideas in this book were developed over 10 years. You also can't count the hours I spent pondering this book in my head, forming the ideas and structure of what you have today. I went into Monk Mode for a few months. I called it that after several people said I was a Monk for how much stimuli I was refraining from. Monk Mode meant a break from movies, TV, YouTube, social media, audiobooks, music, and anything else that pulled my mind away from writing and wasn't necessary to my survival. I had to focus on the goal in front of me, no distractions. Be careful with Monk Mode, though. It can be dangerous. It's like a sprint. You'll run real fast, but you'll also wear yourself out. When you are so singularly focused, things get neglected. Also, ruminating thoughts or unresolved traumas may surface. There is nothing to keep your mind from thinking about everything you've ignored, and there are a lot of people out there with some unfinished business in their closet. You have to be in a strong state to not let your mind destroy you.

I used the mantra 'Every Second Counts' or 'Finish the Book' to bring me back to focus during every dull moment. When I was driving, working out, doing laundry, or grocery shopping, I was still working on the book in my head. It was ongoing mental work.

The initial idea for this book was to document the journey of the neighborhood kid because I didn't know how long I had left. I used to think I might get taken out by a stressor of the *barrio*. I always thought it'd mean getting shot. But instead, I was run over. Luckily, not taken out. I had a chance for a bounceback, and I took it. I honored that chance. I capitalized on that chance. The idea behind the book then morphed into my responsibility to share a neighborhood message, a passing of the baton. I can't meet with everyone from my neighborhood or neighborhoods like it, but I can always just hand them the book.

Writing, editing, and publishing this book took a full year filled with laughs, cries, nostalgia, solitude, gratitude, and deep reflection. As I get older and wiser, I know I will look back on these lessons and honor them for their significance and improve them as I continue to learn this game called life.

This book marks the final chapter of my dominant identity as a neighborhood kid. It will also serve as an ever-present reminder of my responsibility to make my neighborhood a safe and healthy place someday.

I'll always work on making my neighborhood what we dream of, but it'll no longer be my number-one focus, at the cost of my *health* and *longevity*. I will not be ok with sacrificing the joys of my life for the dream of peace in the *barrio*. The accident made me realize that.

The neighborhood kid will always be a part of me. The neighborhood kid's contribution lives on through lasting structures in the community: my nonprofit, the courts, the community center, the leaders I have mentored, this book, the people I have inspired, and the momentum garnered for the neighborhood.

I've moved on from the first quarter of my life's development phase. I'm not a kid anymore. It's time for me to catch my breath and find my next adventure.

Thank you, neighborhood kid, for everything we've been through. You really did something, man. It has been a remarkable moment in history.

I can't wait to see the dreams of the next generation of neighborhood kids.

NOTES

1. Police Chief Robert Luna's Speech: https://lbpost.com/news/lbpd-launches-pilot-program-in-washington-neighborhood-walks-crime-prevention/
2. Gun Violence Response Protocol—Long Beach Activating Safe Communities Final Report: https://www.bscc.ca.gov/wp-content/uploads/2024/06/LB-ASC-Final-Report-Dec-21-2023-Submitted.pdf
3. Long Beach Police Department Door Knocking Campaign—Neighborhood Walks: https://www.longbeach.gov/police/crime-info/neighborhood-walks/
4. Demographics—CX3 Neighborhood Snapshot: https://www.longbeach.gov/globalassets/lbcd/media-library/documents/orphans/cx3/chapter-2-cx3-neighborhood-snapshot
5. Neighborhood Ages & Income—Zone In Anti Displacement Memo: https://www.longbeach.gov/globalassets/lbcd/media-library/documents/planning/zone-in/city-core/zone-in-city-core-residential-anti-displacement-memo
6. English as a Second Language—Cooling Long Beach: https://altago.com/wp-content/uploads/City-of-Long-Beach-Final-Report.pdf
7. Free/Reduce Lunch Rate & Renter Rate—CX3 Existing Conditions: https://www.longbeach.gov/globalassets/lbcd/media-library/documents/orphans/cx3/chapter-3-existing-conditions

8. Emergency Room Visits & Mental Health Reports: https://www.longbeach.gov/globalassets/health/media-library/documents/planning-and-research/reports/developing-a-robust-mental-health-system-in-long-beach
9. Life Expectancy: https://lbpost.com/news/a-tale-of-two-cities-where-you-live-in-long-beach-greatly-increases-your-chances-of-contracting-covid-19/#:~:text=In%20the%2090808%20ZIP%20code%20in%20suburban,per%20100%2C000%20residents%2C%20as%20of%20July%202020
10. Eba Laye—Whole Systems Learning: https://www.wholesystemslearning.org/
11. History of Gangs: https://us.sagepub.com/sites/default/files/upm-binaries/43455_1.pdf
12. Before Crips by Jon C. Quicker & Akil S Batani-Khalfani: https://www.amazon.com/Before-Crips-Discussin-Juvenile-Transgression/dp/1439921989
13. Collective Efficacy: https://www.ojp.gov/pdffiles1/nij/249823.pdf - Higgins, Brian R., and Joel Hunt, "Collective Efficacy: Taking Action to Improve Neighborhoods," NIJ Journal 277 (2016): 18-21, available at http://nij.gov/journals/277/Pages/collective-efficacy.aspx.
14. The Temperature of the Neighborhood—Cooling Long Beach: https://altago.com/wp-content/uploads/City-of-Long-Beach-Final-Report.pdf
15. 14th Street Courts Upgrade: https://lbpost.com/hi-lo/basketball-courts-opening-at-14th-street-park-on-saturday/
16. Pacific City Lights Affordable Housing: https://lbpost.com/news/affordable-housing-provided-for-175-lb-residents/
17. Greenlights is a phrase used by Matthew McConaughey as a way to deem priceless stories/memories in life: https://greenlights.com/

18. "The Mind of Kobe Bryant" Basketball's Life Lessons Video https://youtu.be/kEc4XdQayN4?si=2N9vrymyhd5I-JUmC
19. NCAA Chances of College Basketball: https://www.nfhs.org/media/886012/recruiting-fact-sheet-web.pdf
20. Stage Four Colon Cancer Survival Rates: https://www.cancer.org/cancer/types/colon-rectal-cancer/detection-diagnosis-staging/survival-rates.html
21. Westside Asthma Rates & Life Expectancy: https://lbpost.com/news/business/trade-transportation/residents-get-first-chance-to-speak-on-port-of-long-beach-s-proposed-rail-project/#:~:text=West%20Long%20Beach%20residents%20on,Harbor%20revenue%20reaching%20$15%20million.
22. ACLU Cops and No Counselors Report: https://www.aclu.org/publications/cops-and-no-counselors
23. Ten percent of violent crime: https://lbpost.com/news/washington-neighborhood-safe-streets/
24. Seaside Park Feasibility Study: https://www.longbeach.gov/globalassets/city-manager/media-library/documents/memos-to-the-mayor-tabbed-file-list-folders/2023/march-15--2023---priority-project-funding-requests-list
25. 14 St Courts Vision Plan: https://youtu.be/vFE-HW4b-0F4?si=VoRFVnfWmphX-p5R
26. Traffic Fatalities Vs. Murders: https://www.longbeach.gov/police/about-the-lbpd/year-in-review-and-accountability-report/
27. Safe Streets Long Beach: https://www.longbeach.gov/globalassets/go-active-lb/media-library/documents/programs/safe-streets-lb-action-plan---final
28. Washington Neighborhood Peace Protest: https://lbpost.com/news/washington-neighborhood-residents-protests-for-second-time-against-areas-violence/

29. Washington Neighborhood Street Vendor Protest: https://lbpost.com/news/washington-neighborhood-marches-against-violence-after-robbery-of-local-street-vendor/
30. Washington Residents Call for Pedestrian Safety: https://lbpost.com/news/washington-neighborhood-reignites-calls-for-pedestrian-safety-after-recent-crash/
31. The Rock's Speech: https://youtu.be/n6m2WwysPi8
32. Kung Fu Panda 2 Bounceback: https://www.tiktok.com/t/ZP825U9rh/
33. My Block My Hood My City: https://www.formyblock.org/
34. Water of Systems Change: https://www.fsg.org/resource/water_of_systems_change/
35. Oscar Muñoz-Sanchez: https://lbpost.com/news/crime/fatal-shooting-long-beach-oscar-munoz-sanchez/

READING GUIDE - NEIGHBORHOOD KIDS

How to use this book as part of a curriculum:

Establish the Why

Discuss how this book can serve as a tool for education, empowerment, and engagement. Give examples of life dilemmas and connect them to how this book can create a path toward solving them.

Reading Challenge

Challenge participants to read 1-2 chapters a week and write a short reflection.

Week 1: Intro & Chapter 1

- Why did the author start the book off by talking about his upbringing?
- What's your story?

Week 2: Chapters 2 & 3

- How did gangs shape the author?
- What are the mediums in your life?

Week 3: Chapters 4 & 5
- How did the author view education?
- What did being back make him realize?

Week 4: Chapter 6
- What are some of your favorite projects the author worked on?
- What project are you inspired to start in your own neighborhood?

Week 5: Chapters 7 & 8
- What did you expect after the author devoted his life to helping his community?
- Are there any bouncebacks needed in your life?

Week 6: Chapter 9
- How does this measure up to your idea of making it out? Are there any parts you disagree with?
- How did youth-led walking tours in South Side Chicago reshape the story of their neighborhood?
- What are some ways you can build out your own neighborhood identity?

Week 7: Chapter 10
- What are some beliefs in your community that need an update? What ideas can you replace them with?
- How could you put the frameworks to work?
- What's something simple you can do for your neighborhood?

Week 8: Conclusion & Reflections
- What were the most important lessons from this book?
- What does your ideal neighborhood look like, and how can you make that happen?

Reading Discussion

After each week's reading challenge, break out into small, intimate groups where everyone can keep it real with each other.

1. Ask participants to reference what they remember to engage their recall and to survey the room
2. Use the discussion questions to guide the conversation

Be adaptable when using this book because nothing is universally standardized when applying it to individual experiences. Mix in a flow of fun, humor, tenacity, and inspiration.

Build the next generation of neighborhood kids.

WRITING PROCESS
(HOW I WROTE THIS BOOK)

I've always wondered how to write a book. No one ever taught me. Out of all the books I've read, none of the authors took the time to tell the reader the tactics they used to write their book. I think they missed out on educating their audience on the process. It's time to pull back the curtains on the publishing world. This is for younger me.

Tactics I Used
Phase 0: Brainstorming (2023)
- This is my contemplation journey.
- Should I write it? What would it be about? How long will it take?
- What should you call it? How would you start it? With what stories?
- I am not saying you need to take this long. This was just how long I took. I honestly wish I had moved on the idea sooner. I did way too much pondering.

Phase 1: Writing (April 2024 - Sept 2024)
- 10 Chapters along with subchapters
- I started the writing process on the Notes app for iPhone. It's a user-friendly app that I get excited to open to get in my creative bag.

- I later moved to Google Docs once the Notes app got buggy.
- Whenever I had an idea or felt the writing flow, I would open the app and throw it down.
- I outlined as I was writing. It was hard to create an outline before I knew what meaningful content I should include.
- My best writing flow initiated around the 2-hour mark of a writing session while on my laptop.
- Vision, Environment, Baby Steps: Create a clear vision in your mind of what success looks like for completing your book. Develop a conducive environment for writing and try to eliminate or limit consumption modalities that suck up your time like TV, social media, etc (Mine was movies. I would always try and find excuses to just watch movies instead of writing.). Take small steps every day towards finishing the book. Use the brick-by-brick metaphor to build that wall.

Phase 2: Editing (Oct 2024 - July 2025)

- 20 Personal Drafts:
    1. Read through for missing parts (digital)
    2. Read through for structure (digital)
    3. Read through the content (digital)
    4. Review closely for grammar (digital)
    5. Review data points (digital)
    6. Submit chapters through ChatGPTA for peer review
    7. Use Grammarly for redundancy, grammar, and flow
    8. Read out loud for clarity (digital)
    9. Read in one sitting for cohesiveness (digital)
    10. Submit paragraph by paragraph through ChatGPT for peer review
    11. Read through (physical)
    12. Submit section by section through AI peer review

    13. Read out loud in one sitting (digital)
    14. Read in one sitting (physical)
    15. Read in PDF
    16. Read in PDF
    17. Read out loud in one sitting (physical)
    18. Read in PDF
    19. Read in PDF in one sitting
    20. Read out loud (physical)
- Peer Reviews:
    1. Montserrat Pineda, Public Servant (entire book)
    2. Janice Pope, Educator (first half)
    3. Jared Milrad, Author of *Believe in You* (first half)
    4. Stephanie Chmelik, Public Servant (first half)
    5. Avery Horne, Policy Specialist (entire book)
    6. Eli Romero, Public Servant (entire book)
    7. Julian Cernuda, Public Servant (entire book)
    8. Fern Nueno, Public Servant (entire book)
    9. Jarrod Castillo, Journalist (entire book)
    10. Amir Whitaker, Author of *Escaping the Trap* (entire book)
    11. Leonidas Sloan, Educator (entire book)

Phase 3: Publishing: (June 2025 - Aug 2025)

- Reached out to people I knew who had published a book before.
    - Jared Milrad
    - Vernon Brundage Jr.
    - Mike Guardbasico
    - Tim Graboty
    - Justin Michael Williams
    - Dr. Amir Witaker

- Spent time researching the best ways to publish.
    - Youtube
    - ChatGPT
    - Big 5 Publisher Blogs
- Created a query package: query letter, book proposal, pitch
- Queried 100 literary agents on Query Tracker
- About 20% of the literary agents responded to me, all rejecting the offer, citing the difficulty of selling memoirs for authors without a large following.

Phase 4: Marketing: (June 2025 - Sept 2025)

1. **Pre Launch**
    a. Launch a post announcing the book on all platforms
    b. Daily stories and posts on book details and inspiration
    c. Word of mouth about the book release to friends and colleagues
    d. Announcement with publishing date
    e. Looking back, I wish I had started the process of marketing from the jump. The idea of "Build in Public" is announcing your objectives and timeline to your community and documenting the process. This creates public accountability and builds momentum.
2. **Launch**
    a. Article
    b. Video
    c. Social Media Posts
    d. Community Event
    e. Podcast
    f. Local Press

    g. Program Curriculum
    h. Indie Bookstores
    i.   Elected Officials
    j.   Libraries
    k. Schools

3. **Post Launch (Long-Term Impact)**
    a. Incorporate the book as part of the youth development curriculum
    b. Give out books in the neighborhood
    c. Find a way to honor the message of the book
    d. Provide free online versions for public benefit purposes

REVIEWS

After reading this, leave a review on Amazon, Goodreads, or StoryGraph. The reviews ensure the neighborhood message goes out to a wider audience. Keep it real with me. No need to sugarcoat it.

You can also post about the book on social media and tag me @mcgillsoriano so I can repost it.

Feel free to invite me to your school, nonprofit, team, or program to discuss the story behind the book.

www.ingramcontent.com/pod-product-compliance
Lightning Source LLC
Chambersburg PA
CBHW071113160426
43196CB00013B/2561